Dave McLaughlin

Princeton University 1966
Grace Theological Seminary 1970

*Dooyeweerd
and the
Amsterdam Philosophy*

DOOYEWEERD
and the
AMSTERDAM PHILOSOPHY

by

RONALD H. NASH

ZONDERVAN PUBLISHING HOUSE
GRAND RAPIDS   MICHIGAN

To
BETTY JANE *and* JEFFREY
with love

FOREWORD

During the past fifty years various attempts have been made to establish the connection between philosophy, conceived of as a cognitive discipline, and theology, viewed as a body of religious statements capable of describing the nature of the object of religious experience.

The encounter of philosophy with the Christian religion discloses several basic attitudes toward philosophy. The first is negative to any philosophical tradition developed apart from the Christian revelation. Athens and Jerusalem are thought to have nothing in common; the Christian faith, which is not in need of reason, is itself a substitute for philosophy. Some Evangelicals are in danger of viewing philosophy as something which is of no concern to the believer. Since we have the divinely inspired Word of God, in the Old and New Testaments, it is thought by many well-meaning Christians that the Bible is enough. The answers to detailed philosophical and scientific problems are sought in the Scriptures alone. What need have we of the wisdom of this world when we have the Holy Scriptures?

Christians cannot properly be negative with respect to Christian philosophy. In fact, an Evangelical cannot do without a philosophy. For example, take the well-known and well-loved text in John, "For God so loved the world that He gave His only begotten Son, that whosoever believeth on Him should not perish, but have everlasting life," what does this mean? What does it mean, for example, to say that God gave? Is God unchangeable? How then can we ascribe any action to God? And, as God is eternal how can we speak of Him in terms of past tense? And what does it mean to speak of "an only Begotten Son?" What does the term 'begotten' mean? And, in what sense can God have a Son?

Whenever we use such words as time and creation; whenever we apply names to God and whenever we speak of the relationship between the body and the soul, we are at once plunged into the midst of theological and philosophical problems. To the degree that we do not seek to philosophize in the light of the Scriptures, we are more susceptible to error. It is for this reason that Christians ought to be interested in Mr. Ronald H. Nash's book, *Dooyeweerd and the Amsterdam Philosophy*. For Dooyeweerd's work is a major milestone in the development of Christian philosophy. Between 1926 and the present, Dooyeweerd has been instrumental in the founding of a new movement in Christian philosophy. A rather extensive literature has appeared during these years, the chief of Dooyeweerd's works which were available in English is a four volume work, *A New Critique of Theoretical Thought.** Dooyeweerd has published more than 150 titles and one can speak of a school of Christian philosophers which have rallied around Dooyeweerd as their leading figure. The movement which Dooyeweerd represents is, however, not to be looked upon as a property of a narrow clique of Dutch Calvinists. Dooyeweerd himself would have his philosophy called Christian philosophy without any further qualification.

There is a sense in which what Dooyeweerd represents is new, and yet there is a sense in which it is very old. For Dooyeweerd represents a long standing attitude in philosophy, one which seeks to unite "faith and reason" into a single whole. St. Augustine, for example, held that knowledge is unattainable except by faith, since faith precedes understanding. One does not seek to understand, in order to believe, but one must believe in order to understand. The priority of faith over reason and the necessity of faith for knowledge is an essential feature of St. Augustine's writings and the tradition which he has inspired.

Certain features of Augustine's philosophy have been especially influential on Dooyeweerd. Augustine's entire writings are permeated by single desire: "to know God and the human soul." From contemplating the realities of consciousness, Augustine proceeded to contemplate the world. His interest in the world was always subordinate to his desire to understand God, and his interest in philosophy was always *subordinate to the authority of Christ* which he regarded as superior to reason. The true wisdom is not to be found in the wisdom of the ages

*For a non-technical introduction, see J. M. Spier, *An Introduction to Christian Philosophy*, Presbyterian and Reformed Publishing Co., Philadelphia.

but in the true wisdom which is Christ. A true philosopher, a philosopher faithful to his profession, would recognize Christ, the virtue of God and the wisdom of God, and would not, in the pride of vain science, have revolted from this wholesome humility.

Dooyeweerd is aware of his dependence on Augustine, but he is not satisfied with the latter's failure to clarify the relation between philosophy and theology. Dooyeweerd regards his own position, which seeks to demonstrate the inner point of contact between religion and philosophy, as a recognition of the independence of philosophy, but then, philosophy in a Christian form. Dooyeweerd is a representative of a philosophical trend which has a radical Biblical starting point. For Dooyeweerd, the Christian faith is not to be identified with a theoretical theological system. The true knowledge of God and ourselves *surpasses all* theoretical thought. The true knowledge of God and ourselves, for Dooyeweerd, cannot be a theoretical object of dogmatical theology, nor of a Christian philosophy. It can only be acquired by the operation of God's Word and the Holy Spirit in the heart, i.e., the religious center and root of our true human existence. Such knowledge is therefore the *central pre-supposition* of a Biblical theology, in its scientific theoretical sense, and of a Christian philosophy, insofar as the latter has a really Biblical starting point. This implies that the *central principle* of knowledge of dogmatic theology and that of Christian philosophy *ought to be one and the same.*

It is for this reason that Dooyeweerd finds it impossible to accept the scholastic Thomistic distinction between the natural sphere of knowledge, wherein operates the natural light of reason, and the supernatural sphere, in which our knowledge is dependent solely upon the divine Word revelation.

Theoretical thought, for Dooyeweerd, is always related to the ego, the human self, and this ego is the center and radical unity of our whole existence. This ego is, further, of a religious nature. Therefore, real self-knowledge is dependent upon the knowledge of God.

Without true self-knowledge it is impossible to acquire new insight into the real relation between dogmatic theology and philosophy. Both theological thought and philosophical thought have their center in the same human ego. It is this human ego which is the central reference point of the whole temporal order of our experience. Dooyeweerd thus does not object to Augustine's assigning priority to revelation and to faith, but unlike Augustine he would develop a Christian philosophy in which philosophical questions are not handled within the framework of an elaborately developed systematic theology. Dooyeweerd would subordinate philosophy to revelation (not to theology in a scientific sense), since theology and Dooyeweerd is itself subordinate to revelation, not because philosophy arbitrarily is thought to be the servant of theology, but because a *theoretical analysis of the nature of philosophical thought is able to disclose an essential unity between faith and reason.*

The reality of what Augustine calls the mind, and what Dooyeweerd refers to as the ego, is implicit in every act of knowledge. Dooyeweerd follows Augustine's withdrawal from the external world and seeks truth in the inner consciousness. Philosophy for Dooyeweerd is thought to be impossible apart from critical self-reflection, without which even the external world is unintelligible. "Know thyself" must be rewritten above the portals of philosophy.

Christian philosophy in the past has, according to Dooyeweerd, been a compromise philosophy, and in keeping with what he considers to be the true Augustinian spirit, Dooyeweerd would put an end to all synthesis between Christian and non-Christian thought. The cleft between faith and reason is thus thought to be a cleft between a Christian and non-Christian conception of reason. For Dooyeweerd the Protestant Reformation provided a framework in which Christian philosophy could develop. For, the Reformation viewed Holy Scripture as the norm of theology and philosophy and thus should have led to an inner reformation of the latter. The influence of the scholastic motive of nature and grace was, however, too strong to be overcome by Christian philosophy and Luther, in spite of his confession of divine grace, never escaped the influence of Occamism and he never sought a radical reformation of philosophy itself.

The influence of *Melanchthon* was responsible for the return of the scholastic view of accommodation and during the next centuries retarded the development of a Reformation philosophy by the establishment of a synthesis between the Lutheran faith and nominalistically interpreted Occamism.

Calvin's Augustinian recognition that the *nature of man* has been *corrupted by the fall* and is restored by God's grace in Christ, signified a *break with scholasticism* in philosophy. The special knowledge of faith is buried in the heart, from which proceeds the issues of life. Dooyeweerd appeals to Calvin's essentially Augustinian position that reason has been corrupted; that it not only needed to be healed but to assume a new nature.

This does not mean that Dooyeweerd seeks a philosophical system in Calvin or that he would canonize a philosophical system. But, with Calvin, Dooyeweerd rejects any conception of philosophy which affirms the self-sufficiency of reason and he would relate philosophical thought in its foundation or starting point to the basic articles of the Christian faith, creation, fall into sin and redemption in Jesus Christ.

When Dooyeweerd uses these terms, "creation," "fall into sin," and "redemption" in Jesus Christ, he does not understand them in their *theoretical theological sense*. Philosophy is subordinate, in its starting point, to the basic motives of the Christian faith. Philosophy is not the servant of theology nor is theology the servant of philosophy. Both Christian philosophy and Christian theology are subordinate to a common source, the Word of God.

Dooyeweerd recognizes that the introduction of unnecessary presuppositions into scientific activity is disturbing and damaging to scientific investigation. He is convinced, however, that there are certain presuppositions which are necessary in that they constitute the very conditions under which philosophical activity can take place.

The problem for Dooyeweerd is: how can one distinguish between necessary and unnecessary pre-suppositions in philosophy?

Dooyeweerd's basic thesis that he would defend throughout his entire writings is that even in its own domain philosophical thought is not independent of non-philosophical religious motives. A religiously neutral, objective position is impossible.

The present work of Professor Nash does not attempt to refute Dooyeweerd's main thesis. It seeks to render a "bridge"

between what has already been written in exposition of Dooyeweerd's thought and future explanations.

The critical remarks of Mr. Nash are meant to point out
several problems that need further treatment. A living school
of philosophy requires that its friends and members be con-
structively critical. Mr. Nash's book deserves serious attention
and it is to be hoped that it will direct the serious reader to a
careful study of Dooyeweerd's own works.

The book will have served its purpose if it stimulates others
to take part in the critical study and elaboration of a system of
thought which, "gives important and exciting direction to present and future thought and action and is, in the fullest sense of
the word, a Christian philosophy and a great one."

DAVID H. FREEMAN
Associate Professor of Philosophy,
University of Rhode Island

CONTENTS

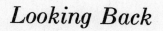

Looking Back

CHAPTER 1

Looking Back

In one sense the history of the philosophy of the idea of law began in 1926 when Dr. Herman Dooyeweerd became the professor of philosophy and history of law in the Free University of Amsterdam. But any detailed study of the historical roots of this movement would have to include stopovers at not only Amsterdam but also at Geneva and Hippo. For in an important sense the beginnings of this philosophy can be traced back from Dooyeweerd through Abraham Kuyper, Calvin, and St. Augustine to the Christian Scriptures.

It was St. Augustine who first made clear the truth, *"Credo ut intelligam."*[1] Many philosophers since him have come to agree that before man can *know* anything he must first *believe* something. It was Calvin who insisted "that man's pre-theoretical commitments determine his outlook in philosophy."[2] And it is Dooyeweerd who today argues against what he calls "the dogma of the autonomy of theoretical thought."

In his inaugural address, Dooyeweerd became involved in general philosophical questions in spite of the fact that he was only trying to find a distinctively Christian foundation for his own field of jurisprudence. He had become impressed with a principle originally suggested by the great Dutch philosopher, theologian, and educator, Abraham Kuyper.[3] This principle, which came to be known as the principle of *sovereignty in one's own sphere*, can be summarized as follows: God has prescribed ordinances or limits for all the spheres or aspects of His creation. Since each sphere of reality is subject to its own God-given laws, no aspect of life has the right to infringe upon the domain

[1]That is, "I believe in order that I may know."
[2]Cornelius Van Til, *Westminster Theological Journal,* vol. XVII (1955), p. 182f.
[3]Kuyper was, in fact, the founder of the Free University, Amsterdam.

17

of any other sphere. While Kuyper had only applied his principle to the relationships between the church, state, home, and school, Dooyeweerd proceeded to apply it to all reality. Finding that no philosopher had given any systematic formulation to the problem of the inter-relationships between the various spheres (which he came to call *law spheres* or *modal aspects*) of the universe, Dooyeweerd and his colleague at the Free University, Dr. D. H. Th. Vollenhoven, have attempted to formulate the principle of the law spheres more fully, as well as systematically develop its implications. Between them they have produced a formidable amount of printed material, the majority of which is in Dutch. The new movement is beginning to grow and is inspiring more confidence as its writings display an increasing degree of clarity.

During the past decade Dooyeweerd's major work, *A New Critique of Theoretical Thought*,[4] has been translated into English. It is being generally regarded as a work of great philosophic importance. Richard Kroner greeted the publication of Volume I by writing,

> One cannot deny that this whole undertaking is as bold as it is urgently needed. The author has a penetrating and subtle mind. He exhibits a stupendous learning in many fields. . . . His system is like that of Calvin, centered in the sovereignty and glory of God, and he is convinced that this central faith is entitled and able to serve as the basis of a new philosophic fabric which would efficiently and sufficiently supersede the defective modern trends of thought. Instead of being unconsciously and uncritically dependent upon a semi-religious creed, this philosophy will consciously and therefore critically admit the inescapability of an original connection between religious faith and theoretical thought, and it will make this inner unity the cornerstone of the whole building.[5]

It is becoming increasingly evident that if one is to keep abreast of contemporary trends in philosophy, he must be acquainted with this new system. However, let no reader think that the only reason why a study of Dooyeweerd is encouraged is simply the satisfaction of one's intellectual curiosity. In his

[4]Herman Dooyeweerd, *New Critique of Theoretical Thought* (Philadelphia: Presbyterian and Reformed Publishing Co., 4 volumes, 1953, '55, '57, '58).
[5]Richard Kroner, "New Critique of Theoretical Thought," *Review of Metaphysics*, VIII (1954-55), pp. 322f.

transcendental critique[6] of philosophy, Dooyeweerd claims to have discovered the true foundation for all theoretical thought which he believes will eventually produce an even greater "Copernican Revolution" in philosophy than Kant's critique of two hundred years ago. Dooyeweerd insists that theoretical thought has certain necessary presuppositions which produce an intrinsic connection between theoretical thought and religious faith. He rejects the doctrine of the autonomy of theoretical thought as a supra-theoretical prejudice.

Dooyeweerd's knowledge of the sciences, mathematics, psychology, philosophy, theology and his own field of jurisprudence makes his work very relevant to present day discussions in these areas. To quote Kroner again,

> It [Dooyeweerd's *New Critique*] fits into the present trend of philosophic thought which has come to realize that the whole modern way of so-called scientific philosophy needs critical reflections and considerations of the most radical nature. The basic relation between religious faith and scientific philosophy can no longer be ignored.[7]

This book has two purposes. Several books have already been published in English which serve as introductions to Dooyeweerd's thought. However, he is still largely unheard of in non-Calvinistic circles. It is my hope that this work may introduce him to many new readers as well as interest them in going to Dooyeweerd's own explanations of his philosophy. But perhaps the primary purpose of this writing is the service it may render as a "bridge" between the already published expositions of Dooyeweerd's thought and what this writer hopes will be more definitive explanations. I have tried to point out several problems that seem to need either clarification or revision. However this book does not attempt to refute Dooyeweerd's main thesis, namely, that scientific and philosophic systems of thought are dependent upon and conditioned by religious or pre-theoretical presuppositions. The problems and

[6]By a *transcendental critique*, Dooyeweerd understands "a radically critical inquiry into the universally valid conditions which alone make theoretical thought possible, and which are required by the inner structure and nature of this thought itself." (*In the Twilight of Western Thought*, p. 4.) In contrast, a *transcendent critique* would not investigate the necessary conditions of theoretical thought. It would rather criticize a particular philosophical argument from another point of view. An example of a transcendent critique would be a Kantian's critique of the Thomistic "proofs" for God's existence.
[7]Kroner, *op. cit.*, p. 321.

inconsistencies that we shall suggest are what one might expect in an undertaking of such scope and complexity. After much independent investigation, I have come to concur with the words of Rushdoony, that Dooyeweerd's philosophy "gives important and exciting direction to present and future thought and action and is, in the fullest sense of the word, a Christian philosophy and a great one."[8]

In accordance, then, with my two-fold purpose, my procedure will be as follows: In the next chapter, I shall attempt to give a brief synopsis of Dooyeweerd's major tenets. One must begin his study of Dooyeweerd as he would that of any systematic philosopher — by degrees. And so my purpose in this chapter will be to present just enough of Dooyeweerd's philosophy to give the reader a general acquaintance with his method, vocabulary, and the content of his system. This chapter will necessarily be general and uncritical since my analysis and criticism will follow in later pages. The reader should look for two basic theories. The first is that "God, the Sovereign Creator, has placed His creation in a cosmic law order. By means of it the coherence between the different aspects and the relations of reality are determined."[9] The cosmic law order refers to a multiplicity of laws that God has established in a regular order. The second basic thesis is that scientific thought rests upon non-scientific foundations that are religious in nature. Pure, unprejudiced thought does not exist.

In the following chapter I shall explain in more detail Dooyeweerd's complex theory of the law spheres. I shall also suggest what seem to be some weaknesses, ambiguities, and inconsistencies in his position. A proper appreciation of Dooyeweerd's analysis of theoretical thought depends upon some understanding of his theory of the law spheres. Then I shall take up Dooyeweerd's doctrine of the Archimedean point of philosophy and his denial of the autonomy of theoretical thought. Finally I shall sum up what to my mind are the major strengths and weaknesses of Dooyeweerd's philosophy.

[8]Rousas John Rushdoony, Introduction to *In the Twilight of Western Thought*, by Herman Dooyeweerd (Philadelphia: Presbyterian and Reformed Publishing Co., 1960), p. xvi.
[9]J. M. Spier, *Introduction to Christian Philosophy* (Philadelphia: Presbyterian and Reformed Publishing Co., 1954), p. 23.

Before beginning, it might be well for us to keep in mind this advice which Dooyeweerd gives in the preface of his *New Critique*.

> This philosophy, to be sure, is difficult and complicated, just because it breaks with much traditional philosophical views. He who will make it his own must try to follow step by step its turns of thought. . . . To those who are not ready in reading to free themselves from the traditional views of reality and epistemology and who look at merely isolated subsections of the work, this philosophy will not open its meaning.[10]

With this good advice before us, let us begin.

---

[10]Dooyeweerd, *New Critique*, I, p. viii f.

CHAPTER 2

The Amsterdam Philosophy

The Amsterdam Philosophy

A good place to begin our analysis of Dooyeweerd's system is with his distinction between "naive experience" and "theoretical thought." Naive experience is the uncritical kind of knowledge possessed by the man on the street. It is a non-theoretical way of looking at the world. The basic characteristic of naive experience is that it sees reality as a whole. Theoretical thought, however, is analytic and antithetic knowledge. It divides reality theoretically into various aspects. Dooyeweerd insists that naive experience and theoretical thought are supplementary ways of knowing and that they are equally reliable within their own domain.

Theoretical thought can be divided into scientific and philosophic thought. Science is always concerned with specific phases or aspects of the universe. For example, if a scientist is a geologist, he studies among other things the structure of the earth; if he is a biologist, he investigates life and living organisms, and so on. In other words, a scientist theoretically abstracts a particular aspect of reality and then concentrates his attention and activity upon that aspect.

But what about philosophy? What aspect of reality does it isolate and investigate? The answer to this question shows the essential difference between science and philosophy. Even though philosophy is a kind of scientific thought, its basic concern is not with any particular aspect of reality but with the entire cosmos, with the totality of reality.

Dooyeweerd believes that the first task of philosophy is the discovery of a proper starting point for its investigation of the totality of reality. Since philosophy is scientific reflection about the totality of the cosmos, it must find a fixed point from which it can view the whole creation. Dooyeweerd calls this fixed point the *Archimedean point.* He is certain that this true starting point for all philosophical reflection must be a part of man because the activity of thinking cannot be divorced from an ego or self which does the thinking. He also argues that the Archimedean point must transcend the cosmos. Dooyeweerd provides a helpful example to illustrate this fact. In the first volume of his *New Critique,* he suggests that if a person wishes to get an exact view of a landscape, he must survey it from a tower or some similar point above the ground. Only from such a vantage point can the various entities that comprise the field, together with their inter-relationships, be seen. Likewise, if philosophy is to survey the entire cosmos and view its divergence and coherence, its fixed point must transcend the universe.

Our author locates the Archimedean point of philosophy in the *heart* or soul of man. He speaks of the heart as the center, the "concentration point," the religious root of every phase of human existence. It is the basis or root of all men's actions. However, care should be exercised not to confuse the heart with any of our vital functions such as faith or feeling.

Whether it realizes it or not, non-Christian philosophy has its foundation in the heart of man, but in a heart that is separated from God. Because man's heart is never neutral, it will either worship the Creator or else turn away from God and deify or worship some aspect of the creation.

> Because that, when they knew God, they glorified him not as God, neither were thankful; but became vain in their imaginations, and their foolish heart was darkened.
> Professing themselves to be wise, they became fools.
> And changed the glory of the uncorruptible God into an image made like to corruptible man, and to birds, and to four-footed beasts, and creeping things. . . .
> Who changed the truth of God into a lie and *worshipped and served the creature more than the Creator.* . . .[1]

Dooyeweerd is convinced that there is one thing about which all non-Christian philosophies are agreed and that is their belief that human reason is autonomous and self-sufficient. He believes that the primary task of a truly Christian philosophy is the destruction of this "idol" of self-sufficient reason.

Dooyeweerd insists that theoretical thought is not autonomous. He argues that "the strictest scientific thinking rests

[1] Romans 1:21-23, 25.

upon non-scientific foundations; that there is an intrinsic and
necessary connection between 'religion' and 'science'...that
there is no such thing as 'pure,' i.e., 'unprejudiced' reason."[2] He
asserts that all the historical schools of philosophy have taken for
granted that their thinking was autonomous, never realizing that
their thinking was actually influenced and prejudiced by motives
arising in the heart. He points out that philosophers have never
come close to arriving at generally the same conclusions and he
believes that they never will until they penetrate to the very
roots of philosophical thought and realize that it has a religious
basis.

Dooyeweerd goes on to note that a non-Christian philosophy can often be characterized by that aspect of the creation
which it worships next to autonomous reason. For example,
materialism "worships" the "idol" of the physical world, empiricism honors sensation as the controlling force in reality, and so
on. Dooyeweerd makes the interesting claim that the acceptance
of his philosophy would mean the final abolishment of all "isms"
from philosophy. All isms such as rationalism, empiricism, materialism, positivism, communism, existentialism, etc., are results
of some man's attempt to elevate one cosmic aspect above all
the others.

Dooyeweerd's name for any philosophy that attempts to locate its Archimedean point within philosophic thought is *immanence-philosophy*. He also has a special name for all attempts
to develop a Christian philosophy by incorporating or synthesiz-
ing concepts from immanence-philosophies into a Christian
framework. He labels all attempts (such as Thomism) *synthesis-
philosophies*. Needless to say, he questions the validity of any
proposed synthesis between immanence philosophy and the
concepts of Scripture. He believes that since immanence philosophy makes erroneous assertions about the origin and nature of
the universe (which are basic questions), its answers to other
questions cannot escape the detrimental influence of its erroneous starting point.

Dooyeweerd proceeds by stating that everything created
either is or possesses *meaning*. By this he intends us to under-

[2]Herman Dooyeweerd, *Transcendental Problems of Philosophic Thought*
(Grand Rapids: Eerdmans Publishing Co., 1948).

stand that the creation is not self-sufficient. He argues that it is important to realize the distinction between God and His creation. This distinction or *boundary* is Law, which accounts for one name of this new philosophy, "The Philosophy of the Idea of Law." God's entire creation is subject to His laws. God's creatures can never escape from the authority of God's Law. "Out of it is exhibited clear as day their creatureliness, dependency, lack of self-sufficiency and incapacity for self-determination."[3] Since science itself is subject to laws (the laws of theoretical thought), it cannot examine that which is beyond the boundary. In other words, God can only be known through revelation.

As we have seen, God made His entire creation so that it is subject to His laws. But there are different kinds of laws. Dooyeweerd has tentatively distinguished fifteen various types. He allows that there may be more, but fifteen is the absolute minimum. He reminds us, for example, that a law of mathematics is not the same as a law of physics. A juridical law is quite different from a law of logic. All the laws which are of a specific nature comprise a *law sphere*. These law spheres must be carefully distinguished from individual things. "These aspects do not, as such, refer to a concrete *what*, i.e., to concrete things or events, but only to the *how*, i.e., the particular and fundamental mode, or manner, in which we experience them."[4]

The terms *law sphere* and *meaning-aspect* are correlative. There are different aspects of meaning in the cosmos. For example, when a person is interested in the price of a thing, he views it from a different aspect or "angle" (in this case, the economic aspect) than if he were merely interested in its beauty (aesthetic aspect) or its age (historical aspect). The number of meaning-aspects is the same as the number of law spheres, fifteen. Dooyeweerd holds that the law spheres are *apriori* inasmuch as they form an unchanging foundation for empirical reality. The law spheres are also ontological. Some have challenged my claim that Dooyeweerd's law spheres are ontological in nature. However, Dooyeweerd makes it plain that the law spheres are not mere categories of the mind or ways of looking

[3] J. M. Spier, *What Is Calvinistic Philosophy?* (Grand Rapids: Eerdmans Publishing Co., 1953), p. 24.
[4] Dooyeweerd, *In the Twilight of Western Thought*, p. 6.

at the world, as Kant held, but have a metaphysical character and actually exist in the temporal cosmos. All phenomena in the created world are based on the foundation of these aspects. It thus seems clear that the law spheres can be described quite accurately as ontological aspects of the cosmos.

There is an order to the law spheres which leads Dooyeweerd to speak of the *cosmic law order*. This order is determined by God and can only be discovered by science. The arrangement of the law spheres is according to complexity, the less complex aspects coming first. Below is a list of the law spheres in the order of their increasing complexity. It should be read from bottom to top.

PISTICAL ASPECT (faith)
ETHICAL ASPECT
JURIDICAL ASPECT
AESTHETIC ASPECT
ECONOMIC ASPECT
SOCIAL ASPECT
LINGUISTIC ASPECT
HISTORICAL ASPECT (culture molding)
ANALYTICAL ASPECT (logic, thought)
PSYCHICAL ASPECT (sensation)
BIOTIC ASPECT (life)
PHYSICAL ASPECT (energy)
MOVEMENT ASPECT
SPATIAL ASPECT
NUMERICAL ASPECT

Special attention should be given to the analytical aspect. It is the "analytical manner of distinction in our temporal experience which lies at the foundation of all our concepts and logical judgments."[5]

This complex arrangement of the cosmos is intelligible only in the light of Dooyeweerd's theory of time. In fact, Dooyeweerd even tells us that the law spheres are aspects of cosmic time. But what can he possibly mean by this enigmatic statement? Its meaning is made clear by three examples Dooyeweerd gives about the relationships between cosmic time and meaning, human experience, and God's law.

[5]*Ibid.*, p. 7.

Dooyeweerd compares time to a prism that breaks light up into its component parts. We have already seen how he believes that the character of reality is meaning, i.e., everything created either possesses or is meaning. But just as a prism refracts light into the various colors of the rainbow, so in the temporal world cosmic time refracts meaning into diverse and yet orderly arrangements of the modes of meaning. It is because of cosmic time that we experience fifteen different modes of meaning. And yet the various meaning-aspects all point to the supra-temporal fullness of meaning which is found only in Jesus Christ.

Consider the example of human experience. In time, human experience displays a great variety of possible functions in our temporal existence so that man can function as a subject in all the modal aspects. Man's subject function in all the meaning-aspects is exemplified by a series of verbs such as I feel, I think, I speak, I save, I admire, I judge, I believe, etc. However, notice that in each case there is an I which performs the function. This helps us see that this diversity of functions is related to the self, the *heart* or soul of man, the religious *center* of his being. In the central unity of his heart, man transcends the multiplicity of his temporal functions.

Consider the example of God's law. Cosmic time refracts God's law into a wide variety of law spheres, e.g., number, space, movement, logic, history, etc. But once again we notice that the several law spheres are all related to the unity of God's transcendent law which Dooyeweerd believes is found in Jesus' words of Matthew 22:37-39.

> Jesus said unto him, Thou shalt love the Lord thy God with all thy heart, and with all thy soul, and with all thy mind.
> This is the first and great commandment.
> And the second is like unto it, Thou shalt love thy neighbour as thyself.

Thus we see that the various meaning-aspects, functions, or law spheres are characteristics of *temporal* reality. But since they are created and thus relative, they all point beyond time to their *supra-temporal* Source or Origin, God.

Time is not enclosed within any one aspect of the cosmos but rather all the aspects are enclosed in time. Thus time and space (one of the meaning-aspects) are not equal and cannot be placed on the same level, as Kant did. Time cuts through and is seen differently in each law sphere. If we picture the law spheres as fifteen charms on a bracelet, time is the chain that runs through them all. This is why Dooyeweerd speaks of cosmic time. Time is expressed uniquely in each aspect. For example, in the first law sphere (number), time is expressed in the sequence of numbers; in the psychological aspect, time is seen as the duration of sensation; in the historical aspect, time is expressed in the periods of history.

Dooyeweerd maintains that each sphere has as its foundation all the spheres that precede it in the cosmic order. The preceding spheres are called the *substratum* and the subsequent ones, the *superstratum*. Although each sphere has a different number of substratum and superstratum spheres, the sum of both the substratum and superstratum aspects contained in each meaning-aspect is the same. This is a cumbersome idea to express but it is really quite simple to grasp. For example, the spatial aspect has only one substratum sphere (number) and thirteen superstratum aspects. The ethical has thirteen substratum and one superstratum (faith) sphere. But the total number of superstratum and substratum aspects is the same (fourteen) in both the spatial and ethical aspects.

Each law sphere has its own *nuclear moment,* which is that basic and irreducible distinction which distinguishes each aspect from all the others. For example, the characteristic distinction of the biotic aspect is life; in the ethical aspect it is love, etc. Also contained within each sphere are *moments* of all the other spheres. *Anticipatory moments* point forward to the superstratum, while *analogical* (or retrocipatory) *moments* look backward to the substratum of the particular law sphere. This is exceedingly important to Dooyeweerd's system. To put this concept in more comprehensive language, within each aspect there are fourteen "points or moments which are representations of the other preceding and succeeding aspects within that law sphere. ... What is the central idea in one law sphere is in all the others a dependent point, characterized by the central idea of the law sphere."[6] This means that each modal-aspect reflects the entire

[6]Spier, *Calvinistic Philosophy*, p. 40.

cosmos through its anticipations and analogies. Since every
modality contains moments that point toward all the other aspects, each sphere is connected with all the others. Thus these
moments constitute an inner coherence between the various
spheres. There is an inner unity to the cosmos and no single
aspect of reality can exist by itself. Dooyeweerd tells us that
false systems of philosophy see this element of truth but err in
then attempting to reduce all the aspects of reality to one. For
example, materialism sees the reflection of the other aspects in
the physical sphere but then incorrectly assumes that the physical aspect is basic and that all the others may be reduced to the
physical.

Closely related to the above remarks is Dooyeweerd's important teaching concerning the *sovereignty of the law spheres.*
According to Dooyeweerd, each sphere is sovereign, i.e., it has its
own individual laws and nature. The capacities of one sphere
are not transferable to any other. This sovereignty of the cosmic
aspects is not absolute since it is derived from the original sovereignty of God. It is also a relative sovereignty since each
particular sphere has its own limitations. The laws of a particular aspect are only valid within the boundaries of that sphere.
To apply this notion to a contemporary issue in philosophy, I
believe Dooyeweerd would agree to a degree with such ethical
Intuitionists as G. E. Moore, Sir David Ross, and A. C. Ewing,
who have asserted the "autonomy of ethics." They have argued
that ethical terms are wholly *sui generis,* that is, ethical terms
cannot be translated without loss of meaning into the terminology of some other domain such as psychology (as is done by
ethical hedonism). I certainly do not wish to press this analogy
too far,[7] but I believe it will help us to understand Dooyeweerd's position. At any rate, Dooyeweerd's concern is not so
much with the terms that are used in any given law sphere as it
is with the irreducibility of that sphere's laws to those of any
other aspect. The laws of ethics cannot be reduced to the laws
of, for example, psychology. However we should understand
that by the phrase "sovereignty of the law spheres," Dooyeweerd

[7]There is, of course, a sense in which Dooyeweerd would disagree strongly
with the so-called "autonomy" of any law sphere. No aspect is autonomous
in the sense of it being self-sufficient. All reality is dependent upon God. Thus,
Dooyeweerd would prefer to use the term "sovereignty" for "autonomous."

is not ascribing any kind of self-sufficiency to any sphere. For him this would be a type of idolatry. It would also deprive the spheres of their meaning and veil the fact that they are meaning-aspects and as such are directed toward God.

When the important truth of the sovereignty of the spheres is ignored, contradictions or *antinomies* are certain to arise. The literal meaning of antinomy is "contradiction between laws." According to Dooyeweerd, the cosmic law order does not contain antinomies. There are no antinomies between the spheres themselves. The cosmos is essentially a unity. Even the distinctions between the aspects are logical. We separate them by "theoretical abstraction," i.e., only in thought. Even sin has not destroyed the harmony in God's law order. Whenever antinomies do occur, they are an indication that someone has either violated the sovereignty of a law sphere or else misunderstood the coherence of the cosmos. For example, the famous antinomies of Zeno (the race between Achilles and the tortoise, the flying arrow) are the result of an attempt to reduce the aspect of motion to that of space. Dooyeweerd believes that—

> By laying bare such antinomies in immanence-philosophy, we apply a method of criticism whose efficiency can be denied only by those who employ a dialectical logic either to overcome the ultimate antithesis in their religious starting point by a pseudo-theoretical synthesis, or to project this basic antinomy as an unconquerable contradiction into temporal reality itself.[8]

J. M. Spier writes in this same connection,

> If a scientist is confronted by two mutually contradictory laws, he can be certain that he has violated a modal boundary and has disregarded the principle of sphere sovereignty. The cosmos is a unity because it has been created. And the scientist can never be confronted by intrinsic contradictions. Such contradictions can be avoided if a scientist strictly observes the laws applicable in his particular field of investigation.[9]

The law spheres correspond to all the aspects of life. For example, the laws of the numerical sphere include the various branches of mathematics. In every sphere there are two sides, the law side and the subject side. In the numerical sphere, the individual numbers are *subject* to the mathematical laws. Dooyeweerd teaches that the subject side of each law sphere also con-

[8]*New Critique*, II, pp. 36, 37.
[9]*Christian Philosophy*, p. 50.

tains the object. This sounds strange, but he is simply trying to explain that both the subject and object are related so that they are under the respective laws of their particular aspects. Any particular thing may function as both a subject and object, but never in the same sphere. Individual things are classified in relation to the highest aspect in which they function as subjects. Hence a stone is a physical thing, a plant is a biological thing, and an animal is a psychological thing (i.e., capable of sensation). Man, however, is the exception to this rule, for he "is the sole creature that cannot be characterized by any specific temporal function. In his heart, he concentrates all temporal functions into a supertemporal state."[10]

Let us consider an example of the above theory. A stone functions as a subject only in the first four spheres. Does this mean that it has no function in the other eleven aspects? Not at all, for in its superstratum aspects, it functions as an object. A sculptured stone may function as an object in the aesthetic sphere; a stone used in the building of an ancient temple may function as an object in the historical sphere; a stone that men value (such as a diamond) may operate as an object in the economic sphere.

Dooyeweerd states that the laws of the first six spheres (number, space, motion, energy, life, and sensation) cannot be broken. But in the remaining spheres the laws are norms that man can break when he so wills. It is man's God-given task to work out and apply the principles of the normative spheres to life.

Dooyeweerd's *New Critique* has many other things to say, especially with reference to sociology. I trust, however, that this brief synopsis has helped the reader to understand and appreciate somewhat the tremendous scope of Dooyeweerd's system. He has developed a philosophy which holds implications for every aspect of life. I believe it deserves our careful study, for in spite of many things we may find unacceptable, we may discover some new solutions to some of philosophy's perplexing problems.

Here is a system which allows us to reopen discussion of some of the traditional problems of philosophy on a new

[10]*Ibid.*, p. 10.

front. Here is a system which promises us philosophies of science, history, language, jurisprudence, economics, etc., which are consistent with each other and with the overarching structure of a world view. Surely such a philosophy deserves our careful consideration.

The Relationship Between God and the Law Spheres

CHAPTER 3

The Relationship Between God and the Law Spheres

In this chapter I wish to examine Dooyeweerd's complex theory of the law spheres in more detail. Before beginning, however, I believe it would be good to consider two warnings that Dooyeweerd gives in his *New Critique*. First he warns us against becoming involved in "problems of the 'philosophia specialis.' This would not only far exceed the scope of a *general theory*, but it would set the reader on a road that he has not yet been prepared for. He would repeatedly come upon general problems that ought first to be looked into in a general theory."[1] Dooyeweerd thus urges us to first study his theory as a whole and then view the particular problems in their relation to his whole system.

Secondly, he warns us about the possibility of confusing a law sphere with an individual thing. He writes, "I must emphatically warn against an identification of organic life as a modality of meaning with a living organism. The latter is a structure of individuality, a typical whole functioning in principle within all the modal aspects alike."[2] Many objections against Dooyeweerd's theories are the result of just such a confusion. I shall try to explain the difference between the theory of the law spheres and the theory of the structure of individuality in chapter 5.

Let us briefly review what a law sphere is. Theoretical thought abstracts reality into fifteen distinct spheres which Dooyeweerd calls law spheres, modalities, meaning-aspects, functions, etc. He calls them law spheres because each area of

[1] *New Critique*, II, p. 107.
[2] *Ibid*, p. 109.

life contains its own distinct kind of law. They are called "modalities because they are ways or modes of existence of temporal reality, aspects because they do not possess independent existence but are features of individual subjects, and functions because they belong to individual subjects that function in time . . ."[3]

Because Dooyeweerd's philosophy purports to be a truly "Christian philosophy," and because he makes it so very clear that the law spheres are created by God, it seems important that we see more exactly what the relationship between God and the law spheres is. However, Dooyeweerd's explanation of this relationship leaves much to be desired in the way of clarity. He describes the relationship by means of a number of extremely ambiguous words and phrases. For example, he tells us that God is "above" the law while the creation is under it; that the law is the "boundary" between God and the cosmos; that God is the "Sovereign" of the universe; that God has "created" the laws; and that everything created either possesses or is "meaning." In order, then, to understand how God and the law spheres are related, we must examine these key phrases in an attempt to determine their meaning in Dooyeweerd's philosophy.

THE BOUNDARY

Dooyeweerd writes that Law is the "boundary between the 'Being' of God and the 'meaning' of the creation."[4] This confusing metaphor has suggested at least three misleading thoughts.

First of all, it has suggested to some that Dooyeweerd denies the immanence of God. Calvinists (and Dooyeweerd is a Calvinist) have traditionally asserted that God is both transcendent and immanent. They avoided any contradiction by distinguishing between the transcendence of God's essence and the immanence of His power. To deny God's immanence would be deism, while to deny His transcendence would be pantheism. Because of the ambiguity of this metaphor, some of Dooye-

[3]William Young, "Nature of Man in the Amsterdam Philosophy," *Westminster Theological Journal* (Nov., 1959), p. 3.
[4]*New Critique*, II, p. 107.

weerd's critics have accused him of leaning towards deism.[5] But a careful reading of his thought makes it clear that Dooyeweerd's use of "boundary" is simply intended to emphasize the fact that God and His creation are not the same. He does not wish to deny the immanence of God at all.

Secondly, the term "boundary" might possibly suggest that a spatial distinction can be made between God and the cosmos, i.e., that they occupy different positions on different sides of some kind of wall (whatever this means). Such a notion is, of course, absurd to any Calvinist such as Dooyeweerd who acknowledges the truth of the Scriptural statement, "God is Spirit." Dooyeweerd wants us to understand that he does not use the word literally. By it he simply wants to refer to that (i.e., the law) which makes a clear distinction possible. God who alone is "above" (this metaphor contains its own problems) the law is to be distinguished from the cosmos which is subject to or under His laws. Spier writes, "When we say that the law is the boundary between God and the cosmos, we simply mean that it divides the Creator from the creation."[6]

Thirdly, Dooyeweerd seems to imply that Law is the only distinction between God and the cosmos. If this is what he means, then he is clearly wrong. Other theists will quickly point out other essential differences. As examples, they could mention the fact that the world is temporal while God is eternal, and while the world is finite, God is infinite. But Dooyeweerd would agree that Law is not the *only* distinction between God and the world. In the words of Spier, "We are not maintaining that the distinction we have made exhausts the difference between God and the creation, but it is of primary importance."[7]

[5]For example, William Masselink has made this objection in his book, *General Revelation and Common Grace* (Grand Rapids: Eerdmans, 1953) and an article, "New Views of Common Grace in the Light of Historic Reformed Theology" (*Calvin Forum*, XIX, 1954, pp. 194-204). In these two writings (which must surely stand as examples of some of the strangest argumentation ever printed), Masselink not only accuses Dooyeweerd of pantheistic tendencies but also of deism. It is possible to see how a man might be accused of *either* deism or pantheism, but to accuse one man of *both* in the same book seems somewhat self-contradictory.
[6]*Christian Philosophy*, p. 33.
[7]*Ibid.*

GOD IS "ABOVE" THE LAW

Dooyeweerd tells us that the creation is "under" the law, while God is "above" it. Forgetting the absurd problem raised by any spatial interpretation of this metaphor, one could easily wonder if Dooyeweerd is ascribing any kind of despotic arbitrariness to God in the manner of William of Occam. Occam, it will be remembered, taught that God's laws were arbitrary and originated not in the divine essence but in God's will alone.

But Dooyeweerd follows not Occam but Calvin on this point. He quotes Calvin's famous phrase, "Deus legibus solutus, est, sed no exlex" which he translates as meaning, "God is not subject to the laws, but not arbitrary."[8] Since God's will cannot act in a way that is in contradiction to His essence, there is an important sense in which God's laws are *not* arbitrary. But this does not mean that God is determined. Whereas it is true that the entire cosmos is subject to divine law and must obey it, God, while not subject to the law, wills to obey it or holds Himself to His own "sovereign" laws. The obedience of the creation is necessary, while God's obedience is voluntary.

GOD IS "SOVEREIGN"

Dooyeweerd writes, "The lex (law) is recognized as originating from God's holy creative sovereignty."[9] Dooyeweerd conceives of God as the Sovereign Ruler of the universe. This metaphor has been objected to on the grounds that it suggests that the universe is organized militarily. This comment (made by philosophers sympathetic to the methods of linguistic analysis) seems somewhat naive. No one, least of all Dooyeweerd, would believe that this metaphor should be interpreted that literally. It is a metaphor and should be understood as such. Faced as we are with the paucity of human language in describing God, "sovereign" does seem to serve a purpose in suggesting the authority and power with which God "rules" or "governs" His creation.

GOD IS "CREATOR" OF LAW

What can Dooyeweerd possibly mean when he tells us that God created these laws? It is possible to conceive how an artist

[8]*New Critique,* I, p. 93.
[9]*Ibid.,* p. 108.

might "create" a masterpiece or how an architect can "create" a new type of building. Many even find no problem with the concept of the "creation" of the world. But in what sense of the word, for example, can a law of mathematics or a law of physics be created? This seems at first glance to be a mixed metaphor that is simply nonsense.

But this confusion results from a failure to distinguish a popular and theological sense of "create." In our popular or ordinary usage of the word, we simply mean that whatever is created has a temporal beginning. In the examples given of the artist and architect, that which their activity produced simply did not exist *before* they created it. But when the theologian speaks of creation, he is talking about something quite different. To say that a certain thing is created (in the theological sense) means that that thing is absolutely and ontologically dependent upon God. Archbishop Temple explained creation as follows: "God minus the world equals God; whereas the world minus God equals nothing at all. You might put it in another way by saying that the universe exists not of itself but only in relation to another whose existence is in himself."[10]

Similarly, since without God there would be no world, so also, without God there would exist no laws. God is the necessary and sufficient condition for the existence of these laws.

THE CHARACTER OF REALITY IS "MEANING"

Dooyeweerd writes that meaning is "the mode of being of all that is created."[11] But what can Dooyeweerd mean by saying that the character of reality is meaning or that everything created either possesses or is meaning? All that he intends us to understand is that the entire creation is dependent and not self-sufficient. The cosmos is relative and only God is absolute. Spier writes,

> Nothing exists of itself, in itself and for itself (except God). Everything exists only in coherence with other things. Every side of cosmic reality points beyond toward the other side of reality. And also, that which is created finds in itself no final point, no point of rest. The whole cosmos points out above itself toward its Creator. . . . But God the giver of meaning

[10]Anthony Flew and D. M. Mackinnon, "Creation," *New Essays in Philosophical Theology*, ed. A. Flew (New York: The Macmillan Co., 1955), p. 173.
[11]*Critique*, I, p. 4.

is not Himself meaning. He is exalted above all meaning, for He alone is self-sufficient. . . . The character of reality as meaning thus indicates its relativity. Only God is absolute.[12]

This is why Dooyeweerd calls the various law spheres *meaning*-aspects. Because the aspects are interrelated, Dooyeweerd speaks of the *coherence of meaning*. No aspect of reality may be isolated from the others. If an attempt is made to do this, "The coherence of reality is rent, a mere abstraction is retained, and God, the giver of meaning, the origin and goal of all things, is lost sight of and is no longer praised because of His works."[13] The *fullness* or *totality of meaning* is found in Jesus Christ.

Dooyeweerd's discussion of this point has raised at least three problems. First of all, he tells us that it is impossible to understand the law spheres apart from their meaning. Then he adds, "If the pre-logical aspects (i.e., those prior to the analytical law sphere) of temporal reality were not aspects of meaning . . . then thought could not even form a concept of them."[14] But Dooyeweerd has already told us that God is not Himself meaning. The question might be raised, then, as to how any knowledge of God is possible. If we cannot understand or form concepts of the law spheres apart from their meaning, how can we possibly have any concept of God?

Dooyeweerd would undoubtedly answer that this problem arises because of a failure to adequately grasp the essential difference between God and His creation. Because the creation is *not self-sufficient*, its meaning can be grasped only when one sees the relationship between the cosmos and the Giver of meaning, God. However, God *is self-sufficient* and an autonomous Being. Because of the limitations of theoretical thought and because He is beyond the "boundary," man can never gain knowledge of God on his own. Knowledge of God is possible, but only as God reveals Himself to man. Admittedly, Dooyeweerd's terminology does raise a problem, but the difficulty vanishes as one looks further into what Dooyeweerd really intended to say.

Edmund Husserl raised another problem when he attempted to reduce theories like that of Dooyeweerd's to absurdity. He

[12]*Christian Philosophy,* p. 20.
[13]*Ibid.*
[14]*Critique,* I, p. 97.

argued that "meaning cannot be burnt down like a house."[15]
Dooyeweerd attempts to answer this objection in his *New Critique*.

> If it is admitted that all the aspects of reality are aspects of meaning, and that all individual things exist only in a structure of meaning, so that the burning house itself, as regards its temporal mode of being as a "thing," has an individual temporal structure of meaning, then HUSSERL'S remark loses all its value.[16]

Dooyeweerd's answer here is anything but clear, but I believe he is saying that it is only particular *things* that can be burnt down and not *meaning-aspects*. It would seem that Husserl's objection rests on the confusion of a particular thing, e.g., a burning house, with the structure of the meaning-aspect that the house exists within.

Because Dooyeweerd is a Calvinist, he must face still a third difficulty. Can sinful reality be meaning? He has defined meaning as the dependence of the creation upon God. But is not sin just the opposite of this, i.e., a rebellion against God? As Dooyeweerd himself asks, "Is it [sin] not meaningless, or rather the adversary of meaning, since meaning can only exist in the religious dependence on its Origin?"[17] Dooyeweerd denies that sin can annihilate the relation of dependence. He believes that "the fullness of being of Divine justice will express itself in reprobate creation in a tremendous way, and that in this process depraved reality cannot but reveal its creaturely mode of being as meaning."[18] This may be so, but a careful reading of these pages in the *New Critique* makes one wonder if Dooyeweerd has adequately explained *how* this is so.

We have attempted to show in this chapter that Dooyeweerd's choice of terms is, at times, an unfortunate one. Some of his words such as "meaning" and "boundary" produce needless difficulties and misunderstandings. Some of his terminology must be accompanied by so many qualifications that I believe his system would surely profit from his adoption of a more explicit and unambiguous vocabulary. I realize that it is not an

[15]*Ibid.*, p. 31.
[16]*Ibid.*
[17]*Ibid.*, p. 33.
[18]*Ibid.*

easy task to describe the relation between God and the world, but it would certainly seem as if Dooyeweerd has made his own task more difficult. Later writings by adherents of this philosophy should attempt to remove some of this ambiguity and vagueness.

*The Relationship Between
the Various Law Spheres*

CHAPTER 4

The Relationship Between the Various Law Spheres

In the previous chapter we attempted to clarify the relationship between God and the law spheres. Now we shall examine in more detail the interrelationships between the individual aspects of the cosmos.

How Is the Number of Law Spheres Determined?

Dooyeweerd admits that his system is not closed and that there may very well be more than fifteen law spheres. He writes,

> In fact the system of the law-spheres designed by us can never lay claim to any material completion. A more penetrating examination may at any time bring new modal aspects of reality to the light not yet perceived before. And the discovery of new law-spheres will always require a revision and further development of our modal analyses. Theoretical thought has never finished its task.[1]

But how, then, does Dooyeweerd know that there are not fewer aspects, i.e., that some of his proposed law spheres are not merely arbitrary divisions of more general aspects? Spier tells us,

> Philosophical analysis of the various areas of reality has shown that these law spheres are indeed original aspects of the cosmos which cannot be reduced to each other. They have their own central ideas which cannot be subsumed under another aspect of reality.[2]

The determining factor, then, in distinguishing any meaning-aspect is the discovery of an irreducible nuclear moment.

How Are the Law Spheres Related?

Dooyeweerd is not very clear on this point. However, he does make two definite statements that provide clues about this

[1]*New Critique,* II, p. 107.
[2]*Calvinistic Philosophy,* p. 36.

49

relationship. He writes in Volume II of the *New Critique*, "The analysis of the modal structure of the spatial aspect will demonstrate that the latter presupposes the numerical one."[3] Later in the same volume, he writes, "The biotic law sphere ...proves to be founded in the spheres of number, space, movement, and energy, according to the cosmic order of time. For the modal structure of the biotic aspect *cannot* exist without these substratum-spheres."[4]

It seems safe to conclude on the basis of these statements that the law spheres are related in the following ways:

1) The lower (substratum) spheres are a necessary, but not a sufficient, condition for the later (superstratum) spheres. For example, the physical aspect is a *sine qua non* for the biotic sphere. While biological organisms necessarily possess physical properties, not all physical properties support life or anything else beyond the physical sphere. However, further reflection about this seems to raise some problems. For example, we are not usually accustomed to thinking of economics as a necessary condition of aesthetics. At first glance, it would seem that Dooyeweerd is talking nonsense if he is trying to tell us that the aesthetic sphere is related to the juridical aspect in the same way that the physical aspect is related to the biological. This difficulty will have to be considered in more detail later.

2) The relationship between the law spheres is transitive. This means that if X is related to Y, and Y is related to Z, then X is related to Z. And so, as the physical sphere is a necessary condition of the biotic and as the biotic is a necessary condition of the psychical, it follows that the physical sphere is therefore a necessary condition of not only the psychical aspect but also of all the post-psychical law spheres.

3) The relationship between the law spheres is asymmetrical. This means that if X is related to Y in a certain way, then Y cannot be related to X in the same way. For example, while physical objects are composed of number (I suppose this means that they are reducible to some quantitative elements), quantitative elements can exist by themselves (as numbers) without being components of some physical object.

[3]Page 83.
[4]Page 107 (italics mine).

Perhaps the reader has noticed that all my examples are derived from the pre-analytical or non-normative aspects. Dooyeweerd's theory, if confined to them, is not too difficult to understand or accept. But the problems begin to multiply when his theory is applied to the post-analytical law spheres.

How Is the Order of the Law Spheres Determined?

Is the order of the law spheres constant? Dooyeweerd believes that it is, and to support his claim he appeals to the increasing complexity of the law spheres as one passes from the substratum to the superstratum. He believes that a critical analysis of each sphere will make clear that it presupposes or depends upon the aspects of its substratum.

I see little reason to question Dooyeweerd's theory insofar as it is confined to the pre-analytical aspects. He is neither the first nor the last philosopher[5] to postulate increasingly complex levels of reality. But when this theory is applied to the post-analytical spheres, the difficulties begin to mount. It seems strange to claim that aesthetics depends upon economics or that the juridical law sphere presupposes the aesthetic.

In order to see how Dooyeweerd deals with this problem, I have arbitrarily selected four of these relationships which I shall now examine in more detail.

1) In what way is the social sphere dependent upon the linguistic? The nuclear moment (or basic distinction) of the linguistic modality is *symbolic meaning*. This sphere includes not only words and letters but also anything that serves to convey meaning. Examples would include such things as signs, flags, and such human actions as smiling or winking the eye. The nuclear moment of the social aspect is *social intercourse*. This is determined when a man comes into contact with creatures other than himself. It seems evident that social intercourse would be impossible if man were unable to first express his thoughts in meaningful symbols. "Every social action, such as a handshake and salute, is necessarily based upon a symbolical

[5]Compare Aristotle's levels of souls in his *Psychology*, Book II. More recent endeavors in this direction include Feibleman's *Ontology* (Baltimore, 1951) and Hartmann's *New Ways of Ontology* (Chicago, 1953). Consider the following statement by Hartmann: ". . . the *conditio sine qua non* of the higher forms of being is always provided by the lower forms, and, in the last analysis, by the entire series of lower forms," p. 36.

foundation. If we greet someone with a kiss or by the removal of our hat, this action is symbolical and signifies or conveys a meaning."[6]

2) In what way is the economic aspect dependent upon the social? In the economic sphere the nuclear moment consists of the saving of *calculated values* or *thrift*. An advanced society uses money as the *measure* of value in economic transactions. Since the value of commodities is determined by human intercourse, Dooyeweerd believes that it is quite clear that economics depends upon the social law sphere.

3) In what way is the aesthetic sphere dependent upon the economic? As we have already noticed, the basic distinction of the economic sphere is thrift or the saving of calculated values. In order for a thing to be an object in the economic sphere, it must be scarce enough for men to value.

The nuclear moment of the aesthetic sphere is *harmony*.

> Everyone who possesses an insight into what is beautiful or harmonious must directly agree that only that is aesthetic which arouses in us a feeling of harmony and is devoid of redundancy and excessiveness. All frills and unnecessary trimming diminish the beauty of an art work. Thus it is evident (sic) that the aesthetic sphere rests upon the economic. Beauty presupposes economy.[7]

However, in spite of Spier's confidence I am sure that many will not find this relationship as evident as he does.

4) In what way does the juridical sphere presuppose the aesthetic? As already stated, the nuclear moment of the aesthetic sphere is harmony, while the basic distinction of jurisprudence is expressed by the term *judgment*, which means primarily, "The well-balanced harmonization of a multiplicity of interests."[8] The word "harmonization" is supposed to indicate the dependence of the juridical law sphere upon the aesthetic aspect.

Much of Dooyeweerd's discussion of the relationship between the post-analytical law spheres seems arbitrary and somewhat artificial. It makes one wonder if Cecil De Boer was not correct when he wrote,

> Perhaps the most unconvincing part of the Philosophy of the Idea of Law concerns the treatment of some of the relations of the ordered levels (law spheres). Many of the so-

[6]Spier, *Christian Philosophy*, p. 85.
[7]*Ibid.*, p. 43.
[8]*Ibid.*, p. 89.

called analogies and anticipations seem a bit thin and far fetched, a defect which the conspicuous farrago of technical terminology does not quite succeed in disguising.[9]

WHAT IS THE DIFFERENCE BETWEEN NORMATIVE AND NON-NORMATIVE ASPECTS?

Dooyeweerd writes that the laws of the pre-analytical spheres "cannot be broken," while the laws of the post-analytical spheres are norms which man can break but which he has the God-given task of maintaining. But this distinction raises several questions. What does it mean to say that the pre-analytical laws "cannot be broken"? In what sense can, for example, the rules of grammar (the linguistic sphere) and of etiquette (the social sphere) be said to be laws of God?

Let me begin by first attempting to make this distinction more clear. In the non-normative spheres, the laws are applied directly by God. The laws exist independent of man. For example, "Anything which has a subject function in the physical modality . . . is directly subject to the law of gravity, even if it is unaware of the existence of this law."[10]

However, the normative laws must be applied directly by man. It is man's task to discover and apply the general principles that God has placed within the structure of the normative aspects. Human activity applies these general principles to reality and makes specific, concrete rules out of them. From these principles man forms concrete rules. Thus any divine content in the normative spheres exists only in principle.

> From the logical sphere onwards the modal laws are only given as regulative principles which cannot be realized on the subject side without rational consideration and distinction. . . . In the pre-logical aspects of reality the modal laws are realized in the facts without human intervention, at least insofar as in this realization the normative anticipations of their modal structure are not concerned. It is an essential characteristic of genuine modal norms that they do not realize themselves in this way. They only offer a rule of conduct to human judgment, a principle requiring *human formation* for its further specification.[11]

But what can Dooyeweerd possibly mean when he tells us that the laws of the non-normative spheres cannot be broken?

[9]Cecil DeBoer, "Calvinistic Philosophy," *Calvin Forum*, XVI, 1951, p. 147.
[10]Spier, *Christian Philosophy*, p. 76.
[11]Dooyeweerd, *New Critique*, II, pp. 237, 238.

It would certainly seem as if errors in mathematical reasoning are violations of mathematical laws. Spier argues against this by trying to hold that errors in mathematical calculation are not examples of breaking a law. He explains, "His (i.e., the man who errs) faculty calculation is a mistake in thought and an offense of the knowing subject."[12] Perhaps what Dooyeweerd and Spier are trying to say can be made clearer by an analysis of the following hypothetical statements:

1) If Jones reasons correctly, then his mathematical calculations will lead him to the right conclusion. If, however, he arrives at the wrong conclusion, we recognize that he reasoned incorrectly.

2) If certain conditions exist, a physical object will fall toward the earth. If an object (such as an airplane in flight) does not fall, we do not suppose that the law of gravity has been broken, but rather, we recognize that the proper conditions were not present.

These examples suggest that there is an important sense in which the non-normative law is not broken. But I am not at all sure if this is what Dooyeweerd and Spier are trying to say.

Let us consider how Dooyeweerd's remarks about the normativeness of the post-analytical spheres apply to one particular aspect, that of history. The nuclear moment or basic distinction of the historical sphere is the *power to form* a culture, i.e., forming an aptitude, structure or situation of a culture into something different than it was or would have been. In history a thing is freely realized in the process of a culture. Although the most important formations of culture are made by the leaders, each person occupies his own place in the development of culture.

There are normative principles of history to which all the formers of history are subject and by which historical formation takes place. Dooyeweerd identifies one of these principles as the call to *dominate* and to *form*. But what is this "call" and how does this call or principle influence history? In what ways is this call known? In what sense of the word can this call be termed a law of God? The answers to these important questions have yet to be made clear. Another principle that Dooyeweerd

[12]*Christian Philosophy*, p. 65.

mentions is the so-called "principle of continuity" which holds that no molder of history can make a radical break with the past. No man has the power to create something completely new, to make a completely new beginning. It is difficult to see why this should be accorded such importance as a principle of historical formation, especially since it seems both psychologically and physically impossible to break completely with the past.

In answer to the old controversial question, "Is history normative?" Dooyeweerd can answer "Yes" or "No," depending on the meaning of the question. If one thinks of history only in terms of the events that have taken place, then Dooyeweerd believes that no factual moment of the historical past can be normative for our conduct today. If, however, by history we understand the historical law sphere together with the principles that "guide" historical development, then history is normative, since the development of culture is governed by historical norms.

Still another example of the difficulties that adherents of this philosophy find in their discussion of the normative law spheres is afforded in these remarks by Spier as he attempts to explain the linguistic aspect.

> Only the principles of language are given. These principles must be specified and positivized in order to become concrete linguistical norms. Consequently the norms of grammar are the results of human work and can be violated by every creature possessing a subjective linguistical function.[13]

But what are these "principles of language" and how do they differ from the concrete linguistical norms? The latter, I suppose, are the rules of grammar and syntax of a particular language. But I have no idea what the former are.

We must conclude that any future writings of this philosophy must attempt to give us a more explicit and acceptable explanation both of the distinction between the normative and non-normative aspects and of the ways in which the post-analytical spheres are normative.

WHAT CRITERION DISTINGUISHES BETWEEN ANALOGIES AND ANTICIPATIONS?

By what criterion can we determine if any given moment is an analogy or anticipation? The reader will remember that

[13]*Ibid.*, pp. 84, 85.

Dooyeweerd holds that each law sphere contains "moments" of all the other aspects. The *anticipations* are moments of the superstratum or more complex spheres, while the *analogies* (or retrocipations) are moments of the substratum. A good example is found in Dooyeweerd's definition of the word "judgment." He defines judgment as "the well-balanced harmonization of a multiplicity of interests." In this definition we can see analogies of the aesthetic ("harmonization"), economic ("well-balanced"), and social spheres ("multiplicity of interests"). By means of its moments, each sphere is connected with all the other law spheres. These moments constitute an inner coherence between the various aspects. To support his theory, Dooyeweerd appeals to such expressions as "vital motion," "spatial image," "thought-economy," etc.

But this raises still another problem for Dooyeweerd. As an example of it, let us consider the phrase, "thought-economy." How does Dooyeweerd know if this is an analogical moment of the analytic sphere appearing in the economic aspect or an anticipatory moment of the economic sphere appearing in the analytical aspect? In other words, by means of what criterion can we distinguish an analogy from an anticipation? Dooyeweerd tells us that in such expressions, there is always one component that qualifies the entire expression, thus indicating that the expression belongs to the same law sphere as its qualifying component. In order to determine which component qualifies the whole expression, we must analyze the expression philosophically. In this way, we recognize that "thought-economy" is not an activity of an economist but of a scientist or theorist. Since the phrase is qualified by its component "thought," the entire expression thus belongs to the analytical aspect and is an anticipation of the economic sphere.

CONCLUSION

Dooyeweerd's discussion of the relationship between the law spheres is one of the weaker elements of his thought. Perhaps the major objection that can be brought against his remarks is that he seems guilty of gross oversimplification. Many of his arguments about analogies and anticipations seem to be invalid by reason of the fallacy of equivocation. As one follows the course of his argument carefully, he finds that the meanings of some of the key terms or phrases have changed. Whenever this is the case, his conclusions do not follow. At other times Dooyeweerd begs the question by defining his terms in a way that will lend support to his thesis. As an example, when trying to prove that the juridical sphere presupposes the aesthetic, he defines the nuclear moment of jurisprudence so that it contains the word "harmonization." This is a disputed definition and I take it that anyone who chooses to define jurisprudence without any reference to the concept of harmonization will not easily be convinced of the truth of Dooyeweerd's position.

I do not suggest that these objections are at all conclusive. I am willing to grant that they may be based upon a misunderstanding or inadequate knowledge of Dooyeweerd's position. My primary goal is to suggest areas of Dooyeweerd's thought to which future discussions of this philosophy will have to pay more attention. And I believe that I have offered some evidence that one of these areas is the relationship which exists between the law spheres.

The Relationship Between Law Spheres and Individual Things

CHAPTER 5

The Relationship Between Law
Spheres and Individual Things

We do not experience law spheres. They are merely theoretical abstractions. What we do experience are individual things such as trees, horses, desks, houses, people, etc. We must now see how Dooyeweerd proposes to explain the relationship between the law spheres and the concrete, individual things of our experience. Although their philosophies were different, the systems of Plato, Aristotle, Hegel and others had difficulty with the problem of individuality. In the *Parmenides,* Plato's Socrates was unable to explain the relationship between the forms and the particulars. Aristotle attempted to locate the basis of individuality in matter. But as Gordon Clark suggests, "Since matter is a virtual non-being and is unknowable, the primary realities, the independent and basic things of the universe are beyond our understanding. And this is close enough to skepticism to make any dogmatist shudder."[1]

Dooyeweerd makes his task even more difficult by announcing at the beginning of his discussion that he will explain individuality without appealing to any notion of matter, substance, or Kantian *ding an sich.* Spier writes, "The philosophy of substance is consequently apostate philosophy. It does not understand God as He has revealed Himself."[2] In fact, Spier tells us that the only way philosophy can discover a correct view of the structure of individuality is to abandon any concept of substance. Thus, it will be interesting to see if Dooyeweerd's philosophy can really present an adequate view of individuality

[1]Gordon H. Clark, *Thales to Dewey* (Boston: Houghton Mifflin Company, 1957), p. 143.
[2]*Christian Philosophy,* pp. 163, 164.

61

while at the same time avoiding any recourse to some underlying substance or *ding an sich* (thing-in-itself).

Dooyeweerd's theory of the law spheres has already been discussed in chapters 3 and 4. It includes his explanation of what the law spheres are and how they are related. The theory of the structures of individuality is concerned with concrete, particular things. Important elements of this theory include Dooyeweerd's answers to such questions as what constitutes things as concrete individuals and what is the basis of individuation? What structure makes an object a unified thing?

THE THEORY OF THE LAW SPHERES AND THE THEORY OF THE STRUCTURES OF INDIVIDUALITY

The basic difference between these two theories is that they are simply two different ways of looking at reality. Each theory investigates reality in a different way. The theory of the law spheres is a functionalistic view of the cosmos, i.e., "It examines them (concrete things) according to their modal or functional coherence. The theory of modalities (or law spheres) is concerned with everything which pertains to the modal aspects, but it does not consider a concrete thing as such."[3] However, the theory of the structures of individuality is an individualistic view of reality. These two ways of viewing the world are not contradictory. The theory of the law spheres is a necessary foundation for the theory of individuality. The theory of individuality enriches our insight into the law spheres and supplements our knowledge of them.

The theory of the law spheres, then, is concerned primarily with the meaning-aspects. Any examination it makes of individual things is only in regard to their relationships to the modal aspects. This theory is not interested in that structure which makes an object a unified thing. It concentrates on everything that is subject to a certain set of laws and notices how, in spite of many differences, these things all have a subject function in that sphere. The meaning of this will become clearer when we notice the relationship between subjects and objects.

[3]*Ibid.*, p. 159.

SUBJECT AND OBJECT

In every law sphere, Dooyeweerd distinguishes three things —the law, its subjects, and its objects. This subject-object relationship has already been mentioned in chapter 2 but it is now necessary to elaborate somewhat on the previous explanation. There are three common theories about the subject-object relationship that Dooyeweerd rejects. A recognition of this difference will better enable us to understand his position.

1) Quite often the statement, "X is the object of Y" is understood to mean "Y knows (thinks about, perceives, etc.) X." This theory identifies the "object" with what is thought about (Dooyeweerd's technical term for this is *Gegenstand*), while the person who thinks is the "subject." According to Dooyeweerd, there is a sense in which all of God's creation is "subject" since it is subject to God's laws. (This looks once again like the fallacy of equivocation!) Dooyeweerd goes on to say that just as there are many things other than thinking men that are subjects, so there are many things that are objects even though they are never thought about by man. For these reasons, Dooyeweerd wants his subject-object relationship distinguished from the traditional epistemological distinction between the knower (subject) and that which he knows (object).

2) At other times the statement, "X is the object of Y" (or "X is objective") is used to mean "X is outside of or independent of Y." This definition identifies any event taking place within man as subjective, while all that is outside of man, i.e., in the external world, is object. But Dooyeweerd finds this usage as unsatisfactory as the first.

3) Finally, "X is objective" often means "X is universally valid." Dooyeweerd objects to this definition on the grounds that only the laws of the cosmos are universally valid and to speak of any object in this way is to confuse the object with the law side of a law sphere.

4) Now let us see what Dooyeweerd's definition of "object" is. First I shall state it in the complex terminology of his system. Then I shall attempt to give a more understandable explanation. For Dooyeweerd, "X is an object" means that "X is an analogical recurrence of an earlier law sphere in a later aspect (or an

anticipatory[4] recurrence of a later law sphere in an earlier one) that assumes a new modal meaning." Since any one thing must, in any given law sphere, be either an object or a subject, X is a subject in any law sphere in which it does not perform an object function.

What does all this mean? Let us consider some examples. A stone functions as a subject in the first four spheres, i.e., it is subject to the laws of number, space, movement, and energy. It does not function as a subject in the biotic aspect (for it does not possess life), in the psychical aspect (for it does not have feeling), in the analytical aspect (for it does not think) nor in any of its other superstratum aspects. Since a thing functions as either an object or subject in any given aspect, a stone's function in its superstratum must then be that of an object. A diamond, for example, functions as an object in the economic sphere. Thus we see that this analogical recurrence of the physical law sphere now assumes a new meaning in the economic aspect. In the physical aspect, the diamond functions like any other stone subject to certain physical laws, e.g., the law of gravity. But in the economic sphere, as an object, it assumes a new meaning as a thing of value, and in the aesthetic sphere it assumes the meaning of an object of beauty. Perhaps another way of stating the difference between subject and object is to say that the subject function is active while the object function is passive.

Dooyeweerd speaks of object functions being either opened (actual) or closed (potential). In "closed situations," things retain their object function, but the function is only potential. In "open situations," the object function becomes actualized. For example, it is possible that we might conceive of a diamond only in regard to its value. In this case, its object function in, e.g., the aesthetic sphere, would remain closed.

The last law sphere in which a thing functions as a subject is important for three reasons:

1) The last subject sphere serves a *qualifying function*. Things are qualified by the last sphere in which they function as a subject. It is for this reason that Dooyeweerd speaks of a

[4]"Analogical" is a relative term referring to any earlier or substratum law sphere, while "anticipatory" refers to any later or superstratum aspect.

stone as a physical thing, a tree as a biotic thing, and a dog as a psychical thing.

2) The last subject sphere serves as the *leading function* of that thing's "internal unfolding process." Spier explains this complicated notion,

> By internal unfolding or opening process we refer to the inner coherence and cooperation that exists between and directs the subject-functions of (e.g.) a tree in the first four modal aspects. It directs them in a certain individual way in order to fulfill a certain end. Whether or not a tree takes nitrogen, lime, or phosphorous as nourishment is indifferent from a modal physical-chemical standpoint. However, in reality, one plant needs more nitrogen. . . . The biotic function leads the unfolding process, as it causes the moments which anticipate the biological aspect in earlier functions to work in a certain manner and direction.[5]

Thus, by means of its leading function aspect, the physical and chemical moments of a tree are guided[6] and lead to certain ends, e.g., nourishment.

3) The last subject sphere serves as the *end function* of that thing. Again taking the example of a tree, we see that the end or goal of the pre-biotic functions is the furtherance of the *life* of the tree.

THE BASIS OF INDIVIDUALITY

As we have seen, everything possesses a modal individuality (as either a subject or object) in every law sphere. A thing retains its identity regardless of how much its law sphere relationships may change. Thus identity and individuality must be based on more than just the modal aspects. An analysis of the functions of a thing is not a complete investigation of the structure of that thing. Spier and Dooyeweerd never grow weary of reminding us that a "thing is more than the sum of its modal functions."[7] The functions arise from a deeper unity. The inner unity of a thing, instead of being enclosed within any one sphere, "binds together all the temporal functions of a thing into an individual structural whole."[8]

[5]*Christian Philosophy*, p. 169.
[6]I should like to point out that it is not at all clear what the words "direct" and "cause" mean in Spier's statement. Is this a conscious or unconscious "directing"? Or if it is neither of these, is it the fulfillment of a divine plan? We cannot really judge as to the truth of Dooyeweerd's views here until we know the answers to these questions.
[7]Spier, *loc. cit.*
[8]*Ibid.*, p. 171.

But what is the basis of this unity or individuality? The closest Dooyeweerd or Spier come to an answer is when they write, "The identity of unity of an individual thing is rooted in the depths of cosmic time...Identity is rooted in the continuous depths of reality."⁹ Overlooking the fact that it may be questionable whether these statements are at all intelligible, they do not identify this source or basis of individuality.

Spier continues, "Theoretical thought cannot penetrate the structure of temporal things...Science must appeal to naive experience in order to grasp the unity of a thing which is in and behind modal diversity."¹⁰ This is surely disappointing. Dooyeweerd assured us that he would explain individuality without making an appeal to any concept of substance. But now that we are finally ready for his answer, Dooyeweerd tells us that there is no answer—or at least that we are incapable of knowing it. Dooyeweerd has been outspoken in his repudiation of Kant's *ding an sich*. But Dooyeweerd's unknown and unknowable basis of individuality begins to look very much like a "thing-in-itself"! John Locke believed that there must be some underlying substance that held the properties of things together. Locke called this substance a "something I know not what." Dooyeweerd also believes that "something" ties the functions of a thing together. But then he stops and claims that this unified structure of things cannot be explained. It is simply grasped by naive experience, that is, this unity is a *given*. One must wonder if there is not another reason why Dooyeweerd stops his investigation where he does. Can it be that he realized that if he went any further, he himself would be involved in the very notion of an underlying substance or *ding an sich* which he earlier rejected as belonging to "apostate philosophy"?

But suppose Dooyeweerd is correct in his assertion that theoretical thought cannot penetrate behind the *given* of naive experience to discover the basis of individuality. Is he, then, not inconsistent in his attempt to refute the concept of substance? How can he be so certain that behind the given structure of individuality which we perceive there is not some underlying substance that does in fact tie the functions of a thing together?

⁹*Ibid.*
¹⁰*Ibid.*

It will be interesting to see if there is any way out of this dilemma. If Dooyeweerd's theory is correct, then he himself is inconsistent in attempting to refute the existence of something whose existence he can neither affirm nor deny. And, of course, if his theory is wrong, it would seem that something in the nature of a major revision in his theory becomes necessary.

The Archimedean Point
of Philosophy

CHAPTER 6

The Archimedean Point
of Philosophy

In this chapter I intend to examine in more detail Dooyeweerd's remarks about the Archimedean point of philosophy.
This is extremely important to his whole theory inasmuch as he
conceives the first task of philosophy to be the discovery of a
starting point for its investigation. My analysis of his teaching
will revolve around his answers to three questions: Does theoretical thought really need an Archimedean point? Why can
this Archimedean point not be found within theoretical thought
itself? and, Why does Dooyeweerd locate the Archimedean
point in the "heart" of man?

DOES THEORETICAL THOUGHT NEED AN ARCHIMEDEAN POINT?

Dooyeweerd's answer to this question begins with a critical
analysis of the very nature of the inner structure of theoretical
thought. An important element of this analysis is the distinction
he makes between naive experience (non-theoretical thought)
and theoretical thought.

> Naive experience is not a *theory* of reality. Rather it takes
> reality as it is *given*, that is to say in its *given structure*. It is
> itself a datum, or rather the *supreme datum* for every theory
> of reality and of knowledge. Every philosophical theory
> which cannot account for it must necessarily be erroneous in
> its fundamentals.[1]

In another passage, Dooyeweerd tells us that in our naive
experience of the world we are not aware of the individual law
spheres. In naive experience,

> We experience reality in the total and integral coherence
> of all its aspects, as this is *given* within the temporal horizon
> of human experience. Naive experience leaves the typical
> total structures of this reality intact.[2]

[1]Dooyeweerd, *Transcendental Problems of Philosophic Thought*, p. 36.
[2]*New Critique*, II, p. 43.

71

In other words, in naive experience we pass uncritically from one domain or aspect of reality to another.

Before attempting to explain these passages, it should be made clear that Dooyeweerd's naive experience is *not* a theory of reality at all and thus should not be compared to such theories as "naive realism" or the so-called "copy-theory" of reality. It follows then that any refutation of "naive realism" is by no means a refutation of the validity of naive experience.[3]

Naive experience is pre-theoretical, i.e., it is not its task to produce theories. "Naive experience is the concrete experience that we have of things and of their relationships with temporal reality in all its fullness."[4] In naive experience, we do not explicitly distinguish the individual meaning-aspects. In a sense, our knowing is in "direct touch" with reality so that we are neither conscious of any difference between reality and our perception of it, nor are we conscious of any distinct law sphere or modal aspect. Naive experience is the kind of knowing that we encounter in everyday life. It is an awareness of reality as a whole, in its totality or fullness. The knower is enabled to conceptualize reality in its fullness without the kind of theoretical abstraction found in scientific thought by means of the subject-object relationship. "Things" exist as structures of individuality in all the law spheres, and it is the existence of these things as either subjects or objects that gives naive experience its integral character. Thus, any awareness of the law spheres in naive experience is merely implicit.

Dooyeweerd denies strongly that naive experience is inferior to or in any way conflicts with scientific thought. The rejection of naive experience as mere phenomenon or appearance which is inferior to the results of scientific investigation is the biased result of the "deification" of science. Dooyeweerd denies that naive experience presents an incorrect picture of reality which science must correct. He argues that naive experience is *not*

---

[3]Dooyeweerd remarks, "It is no wonder that modern philosophical theories of knowledge which hold to the dogma of the autonomy of theoretical thought, were incapable of doing justice to naive experience. Losing sight of the fundamental difference between the pre-theoretical subject-object relations inherent in naive experience and the antithetical relation characteristic of the theoretical attitude, they interpreted naive experience itself as an uncritical theory." (*In the Twilight of Western Thought*, p. 17).
[4]Spier, *Christian Philosophy*, p. 141.

uncritical and unsound scientific theory. He disagrees that scientific knowledge is superior to or more accurate than our naive experience. They are merely two different kinds of knowledge which, instead of conflicting with each other, really supplement the results of the other. Dooyeweerd is convinced that the results of naive experience are, within its own domain, just as dependable and undeniable as the results of science in its field.

> Scientific knowledge cannot be gained without naive knowledge and, the latter is enriched and systematized by the former. Scientific knowledge critically supplements naive knowledge and seeks to control it whenever necessary. In this way naive knowledge is enriched, broadened and systematized.[5]

Naive experience presents no problem for knowledge. The problem of how a person's knowing activity can attain knowledge of reality does not arise here, for in naive experience a person is not engaged in scientific activity or philosophical reflection. But a problem does develop for theoretical thought.

> In science we employ logical abstraction and abstract various aspects of concrete reality. The scientist abstracts the modal aspects of modalities and separates reality into its different aspects. The scientist realizes that feeling is a different function from organic life, and that life is different from motion, and motion different from space.

I find this last remark somewhat puzzling. It certainly seems clear that the distinctions mentioned as examples are just as obvious in naive experience. At any rate, Spier continues,

> The knowing-process in science properly begins with the analytical separation and division of reality. Science separates and distinguishes one aspect from another. The psychologist, biologist, and the historian can only properly investigate the emotive, the vital and the historical function of reality after their respective fields have been distinguished. Each science investigates a specific modal aspect by seeking to discover the way in which its respective aspect is subject as well as the relationships which exist between it and the remaining aspects of the cosmos. The scientist places one aspect of reality as his field of investigation in an antithetical relation to his own analytical function. Scientific thought, is, therefore, antithetical thought.[6]

Thus it is theoretical thought and not naive experience that sets reality apart in the diversity of the law spheres. In sci-

[5]*Ibid.*, p. 133.
[6]*Ibid.*, p. 142.

entific thought (a species of theoretical thought) an awareness arises that there is a distinction between reality (the non-analytical law spheres) and our thought (which is a function of our analytical aspect). Dooyeweerd calls the non-analytical aspects, i.e., the aspects which become the field of investigation for our analytical function, the *Gegenstand*. The problem of theoretical thought is raised by the antithetic relation (*Gegenstand-relation*) between the field of investigation (*gegenstand*) and the analytical function of thought.[7] To summarize this briefly, in theoretical thought we not only oppose our thought (analytical function) to the non-analytical aspects, but we also distinguish the meaning-aspects from each other. "The task of philosophy may be said to be a theoretical regaining of the unity of naive experience, lost theoretically in the abstractions of the special sciences."[8]

It should be clearly understood that unless philosophy can succeed in accounting for the knowledge-yielding synthesis of the analytical function and the *gegenstand*, the special sciences will be unable to justify their claims to knowledge within the particular areas of their concentration. Only philosophy can provide the necessary insight (and we might add, only *Christian philosophy* can provide the *true* insight) into the temporal coherence of all the law spheres.

Immanence-philosophy (Dooyeweerd's name for any philosophy that seeks its Archimedean point within theoretical thought) uncritically accepts this theoretical synthesis as a *given*. It shows no awareness of the deeper problems involved. But reality is not *given* in scientific knowledge. It is *given* only in naive experience. Thus Dooyeweerd believes that "A truly critical philosophy must seek to solve this problem by determining the conditions under which this knowledge-yielding synthesis is possible."[9] In other words, the basic problem of epistemology is the discovery of how the synthesis between the

[7]Dooyeweerd always seems to make this point by means of a very obscure metaphor. He writes, "These non-logical aspects, however, *offer resistance* to our attempt to grasp them in a logical concept and this *resistance* gives rise to theoretical problems" (*Twilight*, p. 8). I am sure that many students of Dooyeweerd's thought would welcome a less anthropomorphic explanation of this "resistance."
[8]William Young, *Towards a Reformed Philosophy* (Grand Rapids: Piet Hein Publishing Company, 1953), p. 102.
[9]Spier, *Christian Philosophy*, p. 143.

analytical and non-analytical functions can take place. Dooyeweerd argues that there must be some point of coherence in
which the analytical aspect comes into "contact" with the
gegenstand. Without such a point of synthesis, scientific knowledge would be impossible. Dooyeweerd poses this basic problem
of knowledge as follows: "From what starting point is it possible
to apprehend integrally in a synthetic view the diverse aspects
of reality which are separated and opposed to one another in
the antithetic relation?"[10] Lest the reader shrug these remarks
off as a mere discussion of methodology, it is good to note these
words by Young: This "is not to be understood as a simple
question of scientific method, as if it were asked where inquiry
is to begin. The primary question concerns the pre-scientific
choice of a position by a man of science."[11]

Almost two hundred years ago, Immanuel Kant asked the
important question, "How is metaphysics possible?" Dooyeweerd is asking today a question that appears to be even more
crucial and critical: *"How is philosophy in the theoretical sense,
as stated above, possible,* that is to say, under what universal and
necessary conditions?"[12] Dooyeweerd is insistent that any denial
of theoretical thought's need for an Archimedean point implies
the impossibility of scientific or philosophical knowledge.

WHY CAN THE ARCHIMEDEAN POINT NOT BE
FOUND WITHIN THEORETICAL THOUGHT?

Dooyeweerd points out that almost all philosophers have
assumed the autonomy or self-sufficiency of human reason.
They have assumed that theoretical thought is perfectly capable
of examining its own presuppositions objectively and without
prejudice. Dooyeweerd argues, however, that any philosophy
that assumes the autonomy of theoretical thought is obliged to
seek the point of synthesis within theoretical thought itself. If
it can be shown that theoretical thought *must* locate its Archimedean point outside itself, it then follows that science and
philosophy are *not* self-sufficient or autonomous.

Immanence philosophy must face the problem of de-

[10]*Problems*, p. 36.
[11]*Reformed Philosophy*, p. 19.
[12]*Op. cit.*, p. 19.

termining which one of the meaning-aspects it will choose as its
starting point.

> There are as many possible theoretical syntheses as reality
> has aspects. There is a synthetic thought of a mathematical
> nature, another of a physical nature, another biological, psy-
> chological, historical, etc.
>
> In which of these possible synthetic points of view will
> philosophical thought seek its point of departure? It does
> not matter which it chooses, for in so doing, it will always
> exaggerate one of these aspects, it will lead to the
> proclamation of the *absolutism of one of the special synthetic
> points of view*. There is the true source of all the "isms" in
> philosophy which haunt scientific thought and furiously give
> one another battle.[13]

Dooyeweerd then proceeds to present several reasons why
such an absolutization of one aspect above the others is wrong.

1) Such an absolutization is pure dogmatism, i.e., it is an arbitrary choice incapable of any sound justification. Any arguments offered in support of such an absolutization are revealed
by careful philosophical investigation to be pseudo-justifications.

2) Such an absolutization breaks the coherence of the
cosmos. It gives undue attention or prominence to one of the
fifteen law spheres, which leads to a distorted view of the cosmos
and its relationship to God.

3) Such an absolutization is a kind of "idolatry." Spier
writes, "To elevate an aspect of reality is to deify it. Non-
Christian philosophy begins by deifying a created aspect."[14]

4) Such an absolutization is inadequate since an investigation of the law spheres has shown that "each field of inquiry
presupposes a theoretical vision of temporal reality which ex-
ceeds the boundary of any particular science."[15] If we recall
Dooyeweerd's comparison between the Archimedean point and
a tower overlooking a field, we see that from this starting point
of philosophy we must be able to survey the coherence and di-
vergency of the entire universe. But if we choose our vantage
point within the diversity of the meaning-aspects, we will find
such a survey impossible. The Archimedean point must in some
way transcend the diversity of the law spheres.

5) Such an absolutization is itself the result of a pre-

[13]*Ibid.*, p. 37.
[14]*Christian Philosophy*, pp. 17, 18.
[15]David H. Freeman, "A New School of Christian Philosophy," *Journal of
Religion* (Jan., 1958), p. 50.

theoretical activity. From what does this act of absolutizing itself issue? It certainly does not issue from theoretical thought! Thus the very attempt to prove the autonomy of thought by absolutizing one aspect is self-defeating since that act itself points to a supra-theoretical starting point. In other words, in order to discover this starting point within theoretical thought, we must still exceed the limitations of theoretical thought.

Dooyeweerd makes an interesting prediction when he writes, "Modern philosophy will have to rise with might and main against our position that this Archimedean point cannot be sought in philosophic thought itself."[16]

WHY IS THE HEART THE ARCHIMEDEAN POINT?

Even if we grant that theoretical thought requires a starting point and that this cannot be found within theoretical thought, Dooyeweerd must still convince us that the heart of man is the true point of synthesis. To do this, he argues that the Archimedean point must satisfy at least three requirements: it must be related to the *arche* or origin of meaning (God); it must transcend the diversity of the meaning-aspects; and it must not be separated from our own subjective self. He attempts to show that only the heart or soul of man fully satisfies all three of these requirements.

1) The Archimedean point must be related to the *arche* of meaning. Earlier we noticed that Dooyeweerd tells us that all created reality is meaning, i.e., it is dependent and not self-sufficient. This followed from his assumption that God is the Creator of all that is. Only God is absolute, and the existence of everything else is relative to God. By *arche* of meaning, Dooyeweerd means the origin of meaning which is the sovereign, holy will of God the Creator.

Before noticing further how the heart of man is related to the *arche*, it is necessary to look briefly at Dooyeweerd's special use of the word "religion." "Religion" should be equated with neither "theology" (which is theoretical, while religion is pre-theoretical) nor with religious activities such as worship (which constitute a particular sphere or aspect of human activities). Religion is universal in scope and thus covers all the various aspects of human life. It is the service of God in every area of our lives. No part of our lives should be lived apart from God. Thus, when Dooyeweerd says that science is based upon religion (as we shall see later), he should not be understood to mean that science is subordinate to theology. Rather, in his broad use of the word "religion," he is saying that the activities of scientific and philosophic thinking must be subject to God who is the Absolute Sovereign over every aspect and activity of life.

The heart is related to the *arche* because it (the heart) is "the religious root of human existence," the supra-theoretical religious root of human nature. Man's relationship to God is determined by the choices of his heart. His heart will either worship the Creator or turn from God and worship some aspect of the creation. There is a sense in which every choice of man is a "religious" choice which is characterized either by reverence (dedication to God) or apostasy (a turning away from God). Every human activity is related to the heart, the center of man's whole experience. Since man's chief function is faith, all his life is religiously conditioned, i.e., faith is always active behind every activity, even the activity of theoretical thinking as performed by the scientist and philosopher. In the words of Freeman, the choice of the Archimedean point is—

> . . . a non-theoretical decision of the full self, a choice of the origin of meaning. Self-knowledge cannot be acquired except by a religious act in which the origin of meaning is chosen. Knowledge of the self and of the origin exceeds the limitations of theoretical thought. Such knowledge is rooted solely in the heart, the religious center of existence. The self is the religious *mode* of existence . . . Philosophy is thus intrinsically connected with a religious act. It (philosophy) cannot be neutral. The proclamation of its neutrality is itself an absolutization of meaning, a religious deed.[17]

Thus the heart of man seems to fully satisfy the first requirement for the Archimedean point.

2) The Archimedean point must transcend the diversity of the law spheres. Before considering this requirement, we must first determine what Dooyeweerd means by the words "transcendent" and "transcendental."

Dooyeweerd borrows "transcendental" from Kant, although our writer applies it to more than just epistemology. By this

[17]*Op. cit.*, pp. 48, 49.

term, Dooyeweerd refers to that which: (1) is enclosed within cosmic time and (2) makes temporal reality possible, i.e., it is basic or foundational to temporal reality. In this sense of the word, the law spheres are transcendental, for even though they are themselves enclosed with cosmic time, they are still prerequisites of temporal reality.

"Transcendent" refers to everything lying beyond the limit or duration of cosmic time. In an absolute sense, only God is transcendent, i.e., beyond the limitations of time. But in another and more limited sense, man through his heart transcends the boundary of time.

The Archimedean point must in some way transcend the law spheres, for if it were enclosed within the diversity of the meaning-aspects, it could not offer a vantage point from which one could view the totality of the cosmos. But even though it must transcend the law spheres, there is another sense in which it must be related to them.

> Philosophy is an activity of the self; it may never be divorced from an ego which functions in the entire coherence of the aspects of the cosmos. The self is not only operative in thought; *it functions in every aspect . . . I* am the central point of reference and the deeper unity which lies beyond and above all the modal diversity of temporal existence. There is, however, *no aspect in which the ego does not function.* Since it is the ego or self which is active in philosophy, a concept of the totality of all meaning cannot be obtained without critical self-reflection. Unless we know what we are, the world is unintelligible. Critical self-reflection is necessary to gain an idea of the totality of the cosmos.[18]

Only man possesses a subject function in all the law spheres. His functions in the post-spatial aspects can be expressed in a series of verbs such as I live, I evaluate, I judge, I love, I believe, and so on. Since the heart both transcends the cosmos and is the concentration point of all man's functions, it is the one point at which the analytical function can be synthesized with the non-analytical aspects.

3) The Archimedean point must not be separated from our subjective self. In his newest English publication, Dooyeweerd writes,

> It is beyond doubt that as long as theoretical thought in its logical function continues to be directed merely to the op-

[18]*Ibid.,* p. 47 (italics mine).

posed modal aspects of our experiential horizon, it remains dispersed in the theoretical diversity of these aspects. Only when theoretical thought is directed toward the thinking *ego*, can it acquire the concentric direction towards an ultimate unity of our consciousness to which the whole modal diversity of our experiential horizon must be related.[19]

In other words, that part of us that is actually operative in philosophic thought is our *self*, and whatever the Archimedean point is, it must be a part of the self.

Dooyeweerd is convinced, then, that there is only one thing that fully satisfies all the requirements of the Archimedean point, and that is the heart of man. In the next chapter we shall see how Dooyeweerd builds upon this argument to complete his destruction of the "dogma of the autonomy of theoretical thought."

[19]*In the Twilight of Western Thought*, p. 22.

*The Dogma of the Autonomy
of Theoretical Thought*

CHAPTER 7

The Dogma of the Autonomy of Theoretical Thought

Dooyeweerd never tires of reminding us that all the historical schools of philosophy have dogmatically assumed that their thinking was autonomous, while it is actually conditioned by religious presuppositions, i.e., it is influenced and prejudiced by motives that arise in the heart of man. It is all too evident that philosophers have never come close to arriving at generally the same conclusions and Dooyeweerd is convinced that they never will until they penetrate to the very roots of philosophical thought and realize that it has a "religious" basis. Dooyeweerd tells us that a criticism of the dogma of the autonomy of theoretical thought "must be considered the primary condition of a truly critical attitude of thought of every kind of philosophical reflection."[1] This is the most important task of a truly Christian philosophy.

Dooyeweerd objects to the dogma of the autonomy of theoretical thought because it is a pre-theoretical assumption. He presents several arguments which he believes should cause us to doubt the value of the dogma as a theoretical axiom. He realizes that while his arguments may not invalidate the doctrine, they should certainly convince us that instead of being a *dogma,* the belief in the autonomy of theoretical thought should become a *problem.*

Dooyeweerd argues that theoretical thought "has in itself no starting-point for the theoretical synthesis. Even here the dogma as to the autonomy of theoretical thought appears to lead its adherents into an inescapable *impasse.*"[2] In order to explain the knowledge yielding synthesis between our analytical func-

[1]*Twilight,* p. 1.
[2]*Critique,* I, p. 45.

tion and the *gegenstand*, theoretical thought is required to seek its Archimedean point outside itself. Dooyeweerd's analysis of this fact which we noticed in chapter 6 not only makes any belief in the self-sufficiency of theoretical thought questionable but it also reveals the intrinsic dependence of theoretical thinking upon the heart of man.

Dooyeweerd also argues that the "dogma" impedes philosophical discussion. He insists that as long as the various schools of philosophy hold to this dogma, they will never realize the true source of their philosophical disagreements. Dooyeweerd makes much of the many disagreements between the contending "isms" of philosophy. They all claim to be founded on theoretical and scientific principles. They all hold to a belief in the self-sufficiency of reason. But if this is so, Dooyeweerd asks, why can they not convince one another by purely rational arguments? He offers as an example the conflict between the Thomist's empirical arguments for God's existence and the supposed refutation of these same arguments by the Kantian. The result of their philosophical conflict is that "these schools continue to follow each its own way after a simulated combat. Have they had real intellectual contact? I believe the answer must be: No."[3] Each system can "prove" the other wrong only because it argues on the basis of its own presuppositions.

Dooyeweerd then raises the crucial question: Are theoretical principles really the starting point of these schools? Or do their theories have hidden roots beneath their so-called scientific principles? Dooyeweerd argues that the latter is the case and accuses philosophers of making the dogmatic and uncritical error of thinking that their pre-theoretical prejudices will pass for universal theoretical judgments that are valid for every form of thinking. Picking on one of his favorite targets, Dooyeweerd claims that Kant's epistemology—

> . . . is based on a complex of subjective prejudices, which are asserted as *theoretical axioms* without their being examined in a critical manner: (e.g.) the prejudice about the autonomy of theoretical thought, that about the spontaneity of understanding . . . as a formal legislator in respect to "nature," that about understanding and sense as the two sole sources of knowledge, and that about the identity of "object" and theoretic gegenstand.[4]

[3]Dooyeweerd, *Problems*, pp. 16, 17.
[4]*Ibid.*

Dooyeweerd insists that one cannot escape this problem by attempting to found epistemology on an ontological basis because ontology, as much as epistemology, is faced with the problem of its possibility. Our author urges us to critically examine the dogma of the autonomy of reason and realize that it should not be used as a scientific postulate. Dooyeweerd sums up this basic thesis in these words:

> In the postulate concerning the autonomy of theoretical thought must be hidden a basic problem of transcendental character, by which it comes to be inconvenient as a starting point for a transcendental criticism of every possible philosophy.[5]

At the risk of repeating myself, I believe it should be remembered that Dooyeweerd is fully aware that his remarks do not prove the impossibility of a philosophical theory without religious presuppositions. But he argues (and well, I think) that the dogmatic claim so often made but so seldom analyzed about the self-sufficiency of theoretical thought should be critically investigated.

Dooyeweerd goes on to insist that this "dogma" is not only a pre-theoretical prejudice, but that there is also an important sense in which it can be described as a "religious" prejudice. David Freeman writes,

> The subjective knowing-activity which takes place in analytical and synthetic thought is not free from a religious root. Scientific thought is religious in its innermost depths. The scientist cannot abstract himself from his science. The scientist is a man. In his heart he has made a religious commitment. He is not neutral with respect to the "facts" that he encounters, for his interpretation of them is prejudiced by the pre-theoretical religious commitment. He believes that they are created "facts" or non-created.[6]

By now the importance of Dooyeweerd's remarks must be clearly manifest. He believes that since the universal acceptance of this dogma has made a real contact between philosophical systems impossible, the unmasking of the supra-theoretical pre-judgments of theoretical thought will, for the first time, make a successful philosophical inquiry possible.

There are two possible difficulties that one may have noticed about Dooyeweerd's remarks. The first is based upon a

[5]*Ibid.*, p. 25.
[6]David Freeman, in a footnote in Spier's *Christian Philosophy*, p. 144n.

misunderstanding but it is worth noticing in order that this confusion may be eliminated. The first difficulty notices an apparent circularity in Dooyeweerd's argument. We are told that all choices are determined by man's heart. "Out of it (the heart) arise all our deeds, thoughts, feelings and desires."[7] But then we learn that one of the most important choices that man makes is his selection of a starting point for his philosophical investigations, that is, the Archimedean point. But the Archimedean point that Dooyeweerd advises the heart to choose is none other than the heart. "Such an Archimedean point is to be found only in the heart or the soul of man."[8] However, this confusion is only an apparent one. Dooyeweerd clarifies it in his book, *In the Twilight of Western Thought*. He writes that the heart—

> . . . is subjected to a central law that we may call the religious concentration law of our consciousness, by which it is obliged to transcend itself in order to find the positive meaning of itself.
>
> Therefore, the real starting-point of philosophical thought cannot be the *ego in itself*, which is an empty notion. It can only be the religious basic *motive*, operative *in the ego* as the center of our temporal horizon of experience.[9]

David Freeman has raised what appears to be a much more serious objection. He points out,

> If a religious motive is in fact universally operative, then Dooyeweerd cannot expect that his own conception of philosophy and of theoretical thought will be free of religious prejudice. He is, therefore, unable objectively to demonstrate that religious motives are intrinsically related to philosophical thought. The introduction of a thesis which in principle denies the possibility of objectivity ultimately makes any kind of demonstration impossible.[10]

However, Dooyeweerd did anticipate this. In his *Transcendental Problems of Philosophic Thought*, which was published in 1948, he wrote, "I do not pretend that my transcendental investigations should be unprejudiced. On the contrary, I have demonstrated (sic) that an unprejudiced theory is excluded by the true nature of theoretic thought itself."[11] But Dooyeweerd's anticipation of the problem does not mean he has satisfactorily answered it. His remarks in this book did not completely meet

[7]Spier, *Christian Philosophy*, p. 15.
[8]*Ibid.*
[9]*Twilight*, p. 33 (italics mine).
[10]"New Christian Philosophy," p. 51.
[11]Page vi.

the type of objection that Freeman makes. In his latest writing, Dooyeweerd again tries to come to grips with this problem.

> This certainly does not mean that our transcendental critique, since it starts from this radical basic motive, may lay claim to a philosophical infallibility. . . . Every philosophical reflection is a fallible human activity and a Christian philosophy has, as such, no privileged position in this respect. It is only its biblical basic motive that can give it a truly Christian character and free it from dogmatic prejudices, which impede insight into the integral order of human experience founded in divine creation.[12]

But in spite of these words, the problem is still there. To be sure Dooyeweerd has given us reasons (and many are convinced that they are good reasons) to believe that the doctrine of the autonomy of reason is a pre-theoretical prejudice. But it would seem that his argument should not end here. There seems to be a good reason to believe that his own thesis, i.e., that theoretical thought is *not* autonomous, may be just as much of a pre-theoretical prejudice. Dooyeweerd seems faced with a dilemma of his own making. He seems to have laid his trap so well that he himself is caught in it. If objectivity is impossible, he should not expect us to take any of his own demonstrations seriously. And if he does want us to seriously consider his own demonstrations, then objectivity must be possible in at least one area (i.e., the conclusions of *his* philosophy). Dooyeweerd cannot afford to accept either "horn" of his dilemma but it is difficult to see how he can avoid the embarrassing implications of this problem.

[12]*Twilight,* p. 54.

The "Heart"

CHAPTER 8

The "Heart"

What is Dooyeweerd's teaching about the "heart" of man? It is evident by now that this is an important and basic element of his philosophy. William Young suggests that Dooyeweerd's theory should interest contemporary philosophers since his attack upon the traditional dichotomy between body and soul—

> . . . is singularly similar to that of the Oxford analytical philosopher, Gilbert Ryle, who has denominated the conception of soul and body as separate substances by the expression: the ghost in the machine.[1]

Dooyeweerd's theory is admittedly difficult to grasp. He tells us that the heart should not be identified with any of the following: (1) man's emotions or feelings; (2) man's intellect or reason; (3) the temporal function of faith (even though it is true that man believes with his heart); (4) nor with any immaterial substance (or material substance, for that matter).

What then is the heart? Dooyeweerd speaks of it as man's self-hood, his human ego, his "I-ness." The heart is described as the concentration point of human existence and the deepest center of our temporal existence. The heart is the point where man is said to transcend time. It is the religious root of man's existence. In this capacity, it is both the source of faith and the source of sin. It is also the source or root of all our thoughts, feelings, and actions.

Man's heart is the deciding factor that determines his relationship to God. Since the heart is never neutral, it will either worship the Creator or some aspect of the creation. Because of the fall of man, the human race is infected with sin. After Adam's sin, "the human heart became corrupt, inclined to all evil, and unable to perform any good . . . Sin lies in the very

[1]"Nature of Man in the Amsterdam Philosophy," *Westminster Theological Journal* (Nov., 1959), p. 7.

depths of our existence, in our religious center."[2] This same truth is expressed in Matthew 15:19, "For out of the *heart* proceed evil thoughts, murders, adulteries, fornications, thefts...." It is the tendency of the human heart to always turn from God. But regeneration, which takes place when the Holy Spirit renews the heart, turns man from apostasy to the worship of Christ.

Some theologians and philosophers have been discouraged with Dooyeweerd's vagueness (some may even be tempted to call it meaninglessness) in describing the heart. However, Dooyeweerd is convinced that such ambiguity is necessary in any description of the soul. According to Spier,

> We must notice that a philosophical anthropology cannot inaugurate a scientific investigation to determine the nature of the structure of the human *soul as the transcendant center* of all our temporal functions. God can only teach us in His Word what the soul is. Science is incompetent to furnish knowledge of the soul. . . . What transcends the cosmic temporal boundary falls outside the reach of science.[3]

To ask for a scientific explanation of the soul would be like asking Kierkegaard for an objective explanation of subjectivity—which is, of course, impossible. Freeman comments on this problem:

> The ego is active in all concept formation, and therefore it transcends a philosophical concept. The self is the concentration point of all my cosmic functions. It is a subjective totality which cannot be resolved or explained in terms of philosophical thought or in terms of any other function or coherence of functions. The self lies at the basis of all its many functions as their presupposition. Self-reflection presupposes that our ego directs itself toward itself. And this return to one's self transcends the limits of philosophical thought. The self which thinks theoretically cannot itself be the result of an abstraction formed by thought. If self-knowledge is to be obtained, the limits of philosophical thought must be exceeded.[4]

But this seems to raise still another difficulty. Earlier we noticed[5] that Freeman wrote in regard to self knowledge that "a concept of the totality of all meaning cannot be obtained without critical self-reflection." But we have just learned that, ac-

[2]Spier, *Christian Philosophy*, p. 117.
[3]*Ibid.*, p. 254.
[4]"New Christian Philosophy," p. 47.
[5]See p. 66 of this book.

cording to Dooyeweerd, theoretical thought cannot give us self-knowledge. Does this mean that the world is therefore unintelligible? Or does it mean that since we are dependent upon God's revelation for our knowledge of the self, an intelligible understanding of the world requires a revelation from God? Dooyeweerd has not made clear which of these is his position. One would suspect that the latter possibility probably represents his position on the matter.

Can we perhaps gain a clearer notion of the soul by contrasting it with the body? Hardly, for Dooyeweerd disagrees with the traditional dichotomy between body and soul. His description of the development of dichotomy in terms of his own philosophy is rather interesting. He tells us that philosophers recognized the power of the logical (analytical) function to grasp the *gegenstand* (field of investigation) in logical universality and abstraction. They then uncritically assumed that the logical function was therefore separated from the pre-analytical functions comprising man's body. Thus the pre-psychical functions were hypostatized into a material "substance," and the post-psychical functions were conceived to be the functions of an immaterial "substance," the soul.

Since Dooyeweerd rejects any form of body-soul dualism, what does he offer in its place? Nothing that is very definite. He writes,

> The human soul is man himself in the structural whole of his temporal appearance. And the human soul, in its pregnant religious sense, is man himself in the radical unity of his spiritual existence, which transcends all temporal structures.[6]

I suggest that this is not at all clear. One becomes a little suspicious at times that Dooyeweerd is an epi-phenomenalist. Take for example this statement from his latest writing: "The mystery of the central human ego is that *it is nothing* in itself, i.e., viewed apart from central relations wherein alone it presents itself."[7] But whether or not Dooyeweerd is an epi-phenomenalist, it will be impossible to judge his theory fairly until he makes it intelligible. Until he does, we must wonder if his proposed alternative to body-soul dualism is really more satisfactory. Some students of his thought are suspicious that the

[6]*Critique*, III, p. 88 f.
[7]*Twilight*, p. 28 (italics mine).

so-called "transcendence" of his heart is only an abstract transcendence. Others suspect that he has not completely avoided the abstraction of Kant's transcendental subject which he has taken such pains to criticize. Dooyeweerd's "soul" is certainly no "ghost in a machine," but one must seriously wonder if it is any less of a "ghost."

I find myself agreeing with William Young when he writes,

> Dooyeweerd's functionless soul, especially when conceived in its separated state after death, seems a more shadowy spectre than the scholastic *anima rationalis* . . . . A heart which includes in itself an element of the functions rather than one which excludes everything functional (i.e., Dooyeweerd's "heart") would after all be more transcendent than the product of pure negation of the functions.[8]

This would seem to be a serious difficulty that more definitive discussions of this philosophy will have to attempt to remove. Until such difficulties are removed, questions will continue to arise about the possible theological implications of Dooyeweerd's theory.

[8]*Reformed Philosophy*, p. 143.

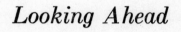

Looking Ahead

CHAPTER 9

Looking Ahead

In this concluding chapter I shall consider Dooyeweerd's philosophy positively (by reviewing some of his more important contributions) and negatively (by summing up some of the major difficulties we have encountered in our study). My remarks are influenced by the primary purpose of this study, i.e., that it might serve as a "bridge" to more enlightening discussions of this new philosophy in the future. Thus any criticisms I shall raise are mentioned only because they reflect my own perplexity, confusion, misunderstandings, or disappointment. They are matters which constitute, I believe, problem areas which this philosophy must take the pains to either clarify or remove.

POSITIVE CONSIDERATIONS

The most promising element of Dooyeweerd's philosophy is, to my mind, his examination of the presuppositions of philosophical thought and his proposed refutation of the dogma of the autonomy of theoretical thought. Dooyeweerd presents some strong arguments in support of his thesis that theoretical systems rest upon pre-theoretical assumptions. A realization of this fact is helpful in understanding the fruitlessness of much philosophical controversy.

There is another aspect of Dooyeweerd's work that we have not had time to consider in this volume. He argues that at different times and in different cultures the basic non-Christian assumption of the dogma of the autonomy of theoretical thought has assumed different meanings. He distinguishes between the form-matter motive of ancient Greek philosophy, the nature-grace motive of Thomism, and the nature-freedom motive of Humanism. These non-Christian religious basic motives, together with the three-fold Christian basic motive of "creation, fall into sin, and redemption by Christ in the communion of

97

the Holy Spirit" have shaped Western civilization. Each of these religious basic motives has at different times acquired definite socio-cultural powers and influenced the structure of Western civilization in many ways. Each culture "is a product of its philosophy and its philosophy is the expression of its religious presuppositions."[1] These conclusions of Dooyeweerd are remarkably similar to those of Pitirim Sorokin, who has shown that if one scientifically studies any culture, he will find that the superstructure of that culture will be based upon a number of basic premises which are philosophical in nature.

Another important contribution of Dooyeweerd's work is his defense of "naive experience." Too often naive experience has been disparaged as being inferior to the results of philosophic or scientific investigation. While denying that naive experience is a *theory* about reality (as naive realism suggests), Dooyeweerd refuses to allow naive experience to be reduced to mere sensory impressions (Hume) or phenomena (Kant). Theoretical thought and naive experience are different kinds of knowledge which supplement the results of each other. The results of naive experience are, within its own domain, just as dependable, reliable, and undeniable as the results of science are in its field.

In spite of its great complexity and numerous internal problems, Dooyeweerd's theory of the law spheres contains many promising implications for philosophy and science. If it can somehow be freed from the difficulties suggested in chapter 3, 4, and 5 of this book, it promises to offer us new solutions to some of the really perplexing problems of philosophy. Dooyeweerd's theory also unmasks the basic difficulty of all philosophical "isms," i.e., they err in attempting to reduce all the law spheres to one meaning-aspect that has been absolutized above all the others.

Dooyeweerd has given us a substantially new critique of Kant. We have already noticed some of his criticisms during the course of our study. Dooyeweerd claims that Kant developed a philosophy that was essentially uncritical and dogmatic because Kant did not have a true transcendental critical

[1]Rousas John Rushdoony, Introduction to *In the Twilight of Western Thought*, p. ix.

attitude. Kant based his theory of knowledge on a number of pre-theoretical prejudices which he asserted to be theoretical axioms without examining them in a critical manner. As examples of these pre-theoretical assumptions, Dooyeweerd mentions Kant's assumption that theoretical thought is autonomous, his assumption that sense and understanding are the only sources of knowledge, his bifurcation of noumena and phenomena, and so on.

According to Kant, antinomies arise when reason refuses to work within the limits of the understanding. Kant recognized four basic antinomies which originate in the abuse of the theoretical, cosmological Ideas of reason which lie outside the scope of all experience. These antinomies each contained two contradictory propositions, a thesis (for example, the world had a beginning in time and is spatially limited) and an antithesis (for example, that the world had no beginning in time and is not spatially limited). Kant believed that the thesis as well as the antithesis of the antinomy were capable of proof, but since they contradicted each other, the antinomies were basically unsolvable. Dooyeweerd, however, asserts that the existence of antinomies indicates that an attempt has been made to reduce the laws or domain of one law sphere to that of another, that is, that someone has violated the principle of sphere sovereignty and misunderstood the coherence of the cosmos. As Spier writes, "Christian philosophy [i.e., Dooyeweerd's philosophy] has developed the PRINCIPIUM EXCLUSAE ANTINOMAE, the principle which excludes antinomies."[2]

Dooyeweerd rejects Kant's placement of time and space next to each other as forms of intuition. For one thing, intuition is a psychical activity. Thus, as Dooyeweerd points out, what Kant really did was reduce space and time to the psychical aspect. Kant therefore misconstrued the true nature of the cosmos. Dooyeweerd also states that space and time are not equal. Space is one of the aspects of the creation while time is seen in all of the aspects (including that of space) in different ways.

Hundreds of pages in Dooyeweerd's *New Critique* contain critical analyses of post-Kantian philosophies on the continent. Many will no doubt criticize Dooyeweerd for his failure to con-

[2] *Christian Philosophy*, p. 49.

sider in more detail the arguments of Logical Positivism, Pragmatism, and the school of Philosophical Analysis. But his critics should remember that Dooyeweerd has lived, studied, and taught on the continent, where these predominantly English and American philosophies have not gained many adherents.

Dooyeweerd's theory of the heart may hold important implications for the mind-body controversy. There seem to be certain similarities between his theory and that of epi-phenomenalism. Both reject (although for different reasons) body-soul dualism. Both agree that any activity of man is an activity of the whole organism. But although Dooyeweerd does not want to be considered an epi-phenomenalist, he has not yet made it clear how his theory differs from that of, for example, Gilbert Ryle. It may be that Dooyeweerd's theory of the heart (for all its ambiguity) is a genuine alternative in the mind-body controversy. But future writings by Dooyeweerd should attempt to state his position more clearly so that the distinctions between his and other theories are more explicit.

Thus, there seems to be much in Dooyeweerd's system that warrants further consideration. His system promises much but, unfortunately, it also has its difficulties.

Negative Considerations

Dooyeweerd's language certainly presents a number of problems. Many times it is an obstacle that one must overcome before his thought can be understood, appreciated, or criticized. I believe we ought to recognize several of the factors that make Dooyeweerd's terminology a problem.

For one thing, this philosophy still is in the process of being developed. A system such as Dooyeweerd's is not completed overnight, nor has it even approached completion in its 35 years of development. Dooyeweerd wrote in the foreword to the first edition of his *New Critique*.

> I am strongly convinced that for the fruitful working out of this philosophy, in a genuinely scientific manner, there is needed a staff of fellow-labourers who would be in a position independently to think through its basic ideas in the special scientific fields. It is a matter of life and death for this young philosophy that Christian scholars in all fields of science seek to put it to work in their own specialty.[3]

[3]I, p. vii.

Dooyeweerd wrote in his foreword to the second edition, which was published in 1953, "Naturally, the evolution of my conceptions has not been at a stand-still since 1936, so that on various points important additions and far-reaching alterations proved to be unavoidable."[4] Many more things need to be said, while still other things that have been said will probably have to be changed.

Secondly, Dooyeweerd, like many of his predecessors, has adopted a new terminology or changed the meaning of traditional philosophical terms to suit his purposes. Thus the reader has to familiarize himself with such new terms as nuclear moment, anticipatory moment, analogy, cosmic time, law sphere, modal aspect, immanence-philosophy, synthesis philosophy, and so on. The reader also has to adapt his thinking to new meanings of such terms as subject, object, gegenstand, Archimedean point, religion, and so on.

Thirdly, Dooyeweerd's philosophy is, in many respects, unique. He does have some new things to say. The reader will recall the warning given by Dooyeweerd in the foreword of his *New Critique,* in which he stated,

> This philosophy, to be sure, is difficult and complicated, just because it breaks with much traditional philosophical views. He who will make it his own must try to follow step by step its turns of thought. . . . To those who are not ready in reading to free themselves from the traditional views of reality and epistemology and who look at merely isolated sub-sections of the work, this philosophy will not open its meaning.[5]

Perhaps the reader is better able to understand this warning now than he was at the beginning of the study.

A fourth reason for the difficulties one encounters because of Dooyeweerd's language is the fact that almost all of the writings of this school are in Dutch. Very few have been translated into English and even those that have, evidence the extreme difficulties of expressing the technical Dutch terms in comprehensible English. There is even disagreement as to how the Dutch title of this philosophy (the Philosophy of the *Wetsidee*) should be translated.

But in spite of these somewhat extenuating circumstances,

[4]*Ibid.,* p. x.
[5]*Ibid.,* pp. viii, ix.

there are still several objections that must be raised about
Dooyeweerd's language. First of all, too much of his thought is
obscured by his vagueness and ambiguity. His discussions about
the law spheres, about cosmic time, about the basis of individuality, and about the heart of man are equivocal and to contemporary Ordinary Language philosophers (and perhaps some
laymen, as well), they are just plain nonsense.

Secondly, there are times when Dooyeweerd's obscurity
seems to disguise real problems. As an example, let us consider
what Dooyeweerd says about cosmic time. He defines cosmic
time as the indissoluble correlation of time-order (past, present,
and future) and factual duration. Gordon Clark, writing in the
Gordon Review, asks if this definition conveys any meaning at
all. Clark points out that for Dooyeweerd time-order and time-
duration are different kinds of time, and that the important notion of cosmic time is a correlation of the two. But since
Dooyeweerd nowhere defines either "time-order" or "duration,"
Clark wonders if it is at all possible to derive any kind of meaning for cosmic time. Commenting on Dooyeweerd's assertion
that there can be no concept of cosmic time, Clark remarks,
"Kant also denied that time is a concept but he at least added
that time is an intuition, which seems clearer than whatever
Dooyeweerd is trying to say."[6]

In this same connection, we tried to suggest that in spite
of his rejection of any notion of substance or "thing-in-itself,"
Dooyeweerd's discussion of the basis of individuality strongly
implies the necessity of such a concept in his system. And of
course many Calvinistic theologians have been wondering aloud
about the implications of Dooyeweerd's doctrine of the heart
of man. Young comments on this problem,

> The heart is certainly not a "ghost in a machine" in this
> [Dooyeweerd's] view, but is it any less a ghost? . . . To the
> question "What sort of 'anima rationalis separata' is left over
> when it is torn out of its temporal coherence with the pre-
> psychical functions?" Dooyeweerd unhesitatingly answers
> "None!"
> Dooyeweerd does not deny the continued existence of the
> soul after death, nor does he represent the state of the dis-
> embodied soul as one of unconsciousness. Yet by depriving

[6]Gordon H. Clark, "Cosmic Time," Gordon Review (Feb., 1956), p. 96.

the soul of its temporal functions, he seems to leave only the most shadowy of spectres in the room of the disembodied rational soul.[7]

Thirdly, some of Dooyeweerd's arguments seem invalid by reason of the fallacy of equivocation, that is, during the course of his argumentation, the meanings of some of his key terms seem to change. An example of this is his discussion of the subject-object relationship and his reasons for rejecting the traditional usage of these terms. He asserts that any use of "subject" (which we shall designate as "S1") to refer to that which knows or thinks about the object is wrong. His reason for this disagreement is as follows: there is a sense in which all God's creation is "subject" ("S2") since it is subject to God's laws. But S1 and S2 are clearly used in two different senses, which seems to make his argument fallacious. S1 designates a thinking agent while S2 refers to the state of being under the power or authority of another. The disagreement seems to be merely a verbal one.

But there are more than simply linguistic problems in Dooyeweerd's philosophy. There seems to be an implicit skepticism (or at least a tendency to skepticism) in his system. Three of the basic elements of his world view are God, the heart of man, and the basis of individuality. And yet in each case, we learn that theoretical thought is incapable of forming a concept of them. Dooyeweerd does make an attempt to circumvent this difficulty. He claims that God can be known through revelation. Christians will have no problem here, but one must wonder if non-Christian philosophers may not consider Dooyeweerd's appeal to revelation a *Deus ex Machina*.

Dooyeweerd attempts to avoid the problem about the basis of individuality by telling us that the fact of individuation is simply "grasped" by naive experience. But this does not say very much, for, on his own view, naive experience only knows that which is *given*.

Of course Dooyeweerd is not the first to state the impossibility of possessing theoretical knowledge about the self. For example, a passage remarkably similar to Dooyeweerd's teaching is found in Arthur Schopenhauer's *The World As Will and Idea*.

[7]William Young, "Nature of Man," pp. 9, 10.

> That which knows all things and is known by none is the
> subject. . . . Everyone finds himself to be subject, yet only in
> so far as he knows, not in so far as he is an object of knowl-
> edge. . . . The subject, on the contrary, which is always the
> knower, never the known, does not come under these forms
> (i.e., those of knowledge, time and space) but is presupposed
> by them; it has therefore neither multiplicity nor its opposite
> unity. We never know it, but it is always the knower wher-
> ever there is knowledge.[8]

But even though Dooyeweerd may be able to justify his
belief that a theoretical knowledge of the self is impossible, he
can still be asked, "If we do not know what the self is, how do
we know that it is the religious basis of all our functions?"[9]

There is another problem that will bother many philosophers, especially those unsympathetic to Christian theism or
those unaccustomed to thinking in terms of the Augustinian
view of faith and reason. I am afraid that many non-Christians
will view Dooyeweerd's whole philosophy as one great *petitio
principii.* Nowhere has he justified his assumptions about God
and revelation. Apart from his presupposition that the cosmos
is a divinely created world order, it might be objected that his
law spheres are only fabrications of his own mind. Freeman
adds that Dooyeweerd's method "introduces a religious concept
of the self before showing that a religious motive is permis-
sible."[10] Thus many of his critics will question the legitimacy of
his introducing religion into philosophy. There is no doubt that
Dooyeweerd can show that questions of ultimate meaning are
related to questions of religion. But Freeman points out that
Dooyeweerd has not and cannot demonstrate that questions of
ultimate meaning are genuine philosophical questions. If one
rejects Dooyeweerd's religious framework, it is impossible to
arrive at the same philosophical conclusions.

> Philosophy is not justified in introducing a theological sys-
> tem which goes beyond philosophical analysis. The traditional
> introduction of pre-theoretical prejudices into philosophy does
> not warrant the continuation of such a practice (i.e., by
> Dooyeweerd). If philosophy is incapable of objectivity, it
> is no longer a cognitive pursuit; it may be poetry, but it is not
> knowledge.

Traditional philosophy may be dead, and Dooyeweerd's

---

[8]In *Philosophy of Schopenhauer,* Irwin Edman, ed. (New York: The Modern
Library, 1956), pp. 5, 6.
[9]Freeman, "New Christian Philosophy," p. 51.
[10]*Ibid.*

critique may help to give its death blow. But, if religious beliefs are arbitrary and if philosophy cannot escape religious beliefs, philosophy ought to re-examine itself and to limit its activity to an area in which objectivity is possible. Such a limitation would not necessarily destroy religion; it would rather make room for it.[11]

In other words, Freeman suggests that perhaps Dooyeweerd's work helps to show that philosophy should be limited to areas where any reference to self-knowledge is not necessary, e.g., mathematical and formal logic.

Inasmuch as it is the purpose of this book to prepare the way for more profitable discussions of this new philosophy in the future, it would seem that some suggestions are in order.

First of all, there should be exerted in all future writings of this philosophy a greater effort to avoid the ambiguity and problems of terminology that are to be found in all of the previous publications. Good thinking is never complimented by and should never be accompanied by poor communication.

Secondly, I believe attempts should be made to come to grips with the objections raised by others and by myself.

Thirdly, I believe that Dooyeweerd's American disciples should extend the implications of his critique of philosophic thought to the peculiar American and English brands of philosophy such as Logical Positivism and the school of the various types of linguistic analysis.

We have yet to hear the last either for or against the Philosophy of the Idea of Law. I trust that this brief study may help point out the directions that future discussions of it should take.

[11]*Ibid.*, p. 53.

BIBLIOGRAPHY

A list of English publications about the Philosophy of the Idea of Law.

PERIODICAL ARTICLES

Clark, Gordon H. "Cosmic Time," *Gordon Review* (February, 1956), 94-99.

De Boer, Cecil. "Calvinistic Philosophy," *Calvin Forum*, XVI (1951), 147, 148.

De Boer, Cecil. "Spirit of Catholic and Calvinistic Philosophy," *Calvin Forum*, XVI (1951), 201-204.

Freeman, David H. "A New School of Christian Philosophy," *Journal of Religion*, XXXVIII (1958), 46-53.

Jellema, Dirk. "Philosophy of Vollenhoven and Dooyeweerd: Part I," *Calvin Forum*, XIX (1954), 169-172.

Jellema, Dirk. "Philosophy of Vollenhoven and Dooyeweerd: Part II. Dooyeweerd and Hartmann," *Calvin Forum*, XIX (1954), 192-194.

Jellema, Dirk. "New Synthesis-Philosophy," *Calvin Forum*, XX (1954), 31-33.

Kroner, Richard. "New Critique of Theoretical Thought," *Review of Metaphysics*, VIII (1954), 321-324.

Masselink, William. "New Views of Common Grace in the Light of Historic Reformed Theology," *Calvin Forum*, XIX (1954), 194-204.

Mekkes, J. P. A. "Philosophy of Vollenhoven and Dooyeweerd (a reply to Mr. D. Jellema, Ph.D.)," *Calvin Forum*, XX (1955), 219-222.

Orlebeke, C. "What Is Calvinistic Philosophy?" *Calvin Forum*, XIX (1954), 139, 140.

Stob, H. "Christian Philosophy," *Calvin Forum*, XIV (1948), 53, 54.

Trap, W. "Scholarly Dissertation Commended," *Calvin Forum*, XVII (1952), 186-188.

Van Andel, H. J. "Calvinism and Philosophy," *Calvin Forum*, XVI (1951), 218.

Widenaas, J. "A Calvinistic Philosophy," *Calvin Forum*, XVIII (1953), 118-120.

Wolterstorff, N. "Christian and Philosophy," *Calvin Forum*, XX (1955), 195-200.

Young, William. "Nature of Man in the Amsterdam Philosophy," *Westminster Theological Journal* (November, 1959), 1-12.

BOOKS

Dooyeweerd, Herman. *New Critique of Theoretical Thought* (Philadelphia: Presbyterian and Reformed Publishing Company).
Vol. I. *The Necessary Presuppositions of Philosophy.* Translated by David H. Freeman and William S. Young (1953).
Vol. II. *The General Theory of the Modal Spheres.* Translated by David H. Freeman and H. De Jongste (1955).
Vol. III. *The Structures of Individuality of Temporal Reality.* Translated by David H. Freeman and H. De Jongste (1957).
Vol. IV. *Index of Subjects and Authors.* Prepared by H. De Jongste (1958).

Dooyeweerd, Herman. *In the Twilight of Western Thought* (Philadelphia: Presbyterian and Reformed Publishing Co., 1960).

Dooyeweerd, Herman. *Transcendental Problems of Philosophic Thought* (Grand Rapids: Eerdmans, 1953).

Masselink, William. *General Revelation and Common Grace* (Grand Rapids: Eerdmans, 1953).

Spier, J. M. *Introduction to Christian Philosophy* (Philadelphia: Presbyterian and Reformed, 1954).

Spier, J. M. *What Is Calvinistic Philosophy?* (Grand Rapids: Eerdmans, 1953).

Young, William. *Towards a Reformed Philosophy* (Grand Rapids: Erdmans, 1953).

INDEX

A

aesthetic aspect — 28, 34, 50, 52, 57, 64
analogical moments — 31f, 53, 55f, 63f
analytical aspect — 29, 44, 64, 74f, 79, 83f, 92
analytical philosophy — 42, 91, 100, 105
anticipatory moments — 31f, 53, 55f, 63f
antinomies — 33, 99
anti-thetical relation — 72n, 73, 74
arché — 77f
archimedean point — 20, 26, 27, 71-80, 84, 86
Aristotle — 51, 61
aspect (see law sphere)
Augustine of Hippo — 17, 104
"autonomy of ethics" — 32
autonomy of theoretical thought — 19, 20, 26, 27, 75, 77, 80, 83-87, 97, 99

B

biotic aspect — 31, 50, 64, 65
body and soul — 91ff, 100
"boundary" — 28, 33, 40f

C

Calvin, John — 17, 42.
Calvinism — 40f, 45, 102
Clark, Gordon — 61, 102
"closed situations" — 64
coherence of cosmos — 20, 26, 33, 55, 61, 71, 76, 79
coherence of meaning — 44
contradiction — 33
"Copernican Revolution" — 19
cosmic law order — 20, 29, 33
cosmic time — 29ff, 50, 66, 79, 102
cosmos — 26, 28, 29, 30, 31, 32, 41, 44, 63, 79, 104
creation — 20, 26, 28, 40, 41, 44, 63, 97
Creator — 26, 41, 42f, 77, 78, 91
culture — 54, 55, 97

D

De Boer, Cecil — 52
deism — 40, 41n
ding-an-sich — 61, 62, 66

E

economic aspect — 34, 50, 52, 64
ego — 26, 30, 79, 80, 86, 91, 92

epi-phenomenalism — 92, 100
epistemology — 71-80, 85
ethical aspects — 31
Ewing, A. C. — 32

F

faith — 18, 19, 26, 78, 91, 104
fallacy —
 of begging the question — 56
 of equivocation — 56, 63, 103
Freeman, David H. — 78, 85, 86, 87, 92, 104, 105
Free University — 17, 18
fullness of meaning — 44
function —
 end — 65
 leading — 65
 qualifying — 64f
functions — 26, 30, 34, 38, 61, 66, 79, 92

G

gegenstand — 63, 74f, 84, 93
gegenstand-relation — 74
"ghost in the machine" — 91, 94, 102
God — 20, 26, 28, 29, 30, 39-46, 53, 54, 61, 77, 78, 79, 84, 91, 93, 103, 104

H

Hartman, Nicolai — 51n
heart, the — 26, 27, 34, 71-80, 84, 85, 86, 91-94, 100, 102, 103
Hegel, G. W. F. — 61
historical aspect — 28, 31, 34, 54ff
Hume, David — 98
Husserl, Edmund — 44f

I

idolatry — 33, 76
immanence of God — 40f
immanence-philosophy — 27, 33
individuality — 28, 39, 45, 61-67, 72, 103
In the Twilight of Western Thought — 79f, 86
Intuitionism, ethical — 32

J

Jesus Christ — 30, 44, 92
juridical aspect — 50, 52, 57

K

Kant, Immanuel — 19, 29, 31, 61, 66, 75, 78, 84, 94, 98f, 102
Kantianism — 19, 84
Kierkegaard, Soren — 92

107